[illegible]
1981

THE LAW AND THE PROFITS

By C. Northcote Parkinson

Parkinson's Law

The Evolution of Political Thought

The Law and the Profits

BY C. NORTHCOTE PARKINSON

THE LAW AND THE PROFITS

Illustrated by Robert C. Osborn

HOUGHTON MIFFLIN COMPANY BOSTON
The Riverside Press Cambridge
1960

First Printing

Library of Congress Catalog Card
Number: 60-5152

Printed in the U.S.A.

for Charles and Antonia

PREFACE

THE first purpose of this book is to show that there are limits to the collection of revenue and that evils multiply when these limits are ignored. There is a law by which public expenditure is governed and obedience to this law is universal, eternal and all but inevitable. The existence of this law needs to be widely recognized, and its recognition would imply a revolution in public finance.

The second purpose of this book is to show that a greatly reduced revenue would bring about an improvement, not a decline, in the public services. It is the paradox of administration that fewer people have less to do and more time, therefore, in which to think about what they are doing. When funds are limitless, the only economy made is in thinking. The worst inefficiencies do not stem from a lack of funds but from an initial failure to decide exactly what the object is. It is this muddled thinking that leads to waste, and often to waste on a colossal scale. Toward eliminating public waste an essential step is to reduce the total revenue. Officials are less inclined to squander what is not there. A knowledge of the law which governs expenditure should ensure that the profits from taxation are seldom thrown away.

I would wish to express my thanks to all those who have sent me information and encouragement. With great reluctance I have decided to name no one of them. To include all would be impossible, for some prefer, and with good reason, to remain anonymous. To list the remainder would still mean printing a whole page in which the names of the active and influential would be mingled with those of the merely sympathetic or aggrieved; and yet it would be invidious to distinguish some correspondents and relegate others to oblivion. Faced with these difficulties of choice, I have decided to mention none but express my thanks to all. Without the generous help of many people personally unknown to me, this book would have had a far narrower basis of experience and fact. They are in no way responsible for any shortcomings in accuracy, still less for any of the opinions expressed, but I am deeply grateful for their help. The only allies I shall name individually are my American publishers, who have been unfailingly helpful, Robert Osborn who did the illustrations, Mrs. Sykes who typed the manuscript, and my wife to whom, as always, I owe so much.

C. Northcote Parkinson

Department of Political Science
University of Illinois

CONTENTS

1

PARKINSON'S SECOND LAW

An extremely wealthy man underwent an extremely serious operation at the hands of an extremely distinguished surgeon. Ten days afterwards the surgeon asked how his patient was progressing. "Doing fine," said the nurse. "He has already been trying to date Nurse Audrey, a sure sign of convalescence."

"Nurse Audrey?" asked the surgeon quickly. "Is that the blond girl from Illinois?"

"No," the nurse assured him, "Nurse Audrey is the redhead from Missouri."

"In that case," said the surgeon, "the patient needs something to steady his pulse. I shall tell him what the operation cost."

The patient sobered down under this treatment and did some rapid calculations on the back of his temperature chart.

"Your fee of $4000," he finally concluded, "represents

the proportion I retain from the last $44,500 of my income. To pay you without being worse off would mean earning another $44,500 more than last year; no easy task."

"Well," replied the surgeon, "you know how it is. It is only by charging you that much that I can afford to charge others little or nothing."

"No doubt," said the patient. "But the fee still absorbs $44,500 of my theoretical income — no inconsiderable sum. Might I ask what proportion of the $4000 you will manage to retain?"

It was the surgeon's turn to scribble calculations, as a result of which he concluded that his actual gain, after tax had been paid, would amount to $800.

"Allow me to observe," said the patient, "that I must therefore earn $44,500 in order to give you $800 of spendable income; the entire balance going to government. Does that strike you as a transaction profitable to either of us?"

"Well, frankly, no," admitted the surgeon. "Put like that, the whole thing is absurd. But what else can we do?"

"First, we can make certain that no one is listening. No one at the keyhole? No federal agent under the bed? No tape recorder in the — ? Are you quite sure that we can keep this strictly to ourselves?"

"Quite sure," the surgeon replied after quickly opening the door and glancing up and down the corridor. "What do you suggest?"

"Come closer so that I can whisper. *Why don't I give you a case of Scotch and so call it quits?*"

"Not enough," hissed the surgeon, "but if you made it *two* cases . . . ?"

"Yes?" whispered the patient.

"And lent me your cabin cruiser for three weeks in September . . ."

"*Yes?*"

"We might call it a deal!"

"That's fine. And do you know what gave me the idea? I studied Parkinson's Law and realized that excessive taxation has made nonsense of everything!"

"Rubbish, my dear fellow. Parkinson's Law has nothing to do with taxation. It has to do with overstaffing — of which, by the way, this hospital provides some interesting examples. In parasitology, for — "

"Like all medical men, you are out of date. You are referring to Parkinson's *First* Law. I am referring to his *Second* Law."

"I must admit that I never heard of it. It concerns taxation, you say?"

"It concerns taxation. It also concerns you. Now, listen . . . listen carefully. *Expenditure rises to meet income!*"

Expenditure rises to meet income. Parkinson's Second Law, like the first, is a matter of everyday experience, manifest as soon as it is stated, as obvious as it is simple. When the individual has a raise in salary, he and his wife are prone to decide how the additional income is to be spent; so much on an insurance policy, so much to the savings bank, so much in a trust fund for the children. They might just as well save themselves the trouble, for no surplus ever comes into view. The extra salary is silently absorbed, leaving the family barely in credit and often, in fact, with a deficit which has actually increased. Individual expenditure not only rises to meet income but tends to surpass it, and probably always will.

It is less widely recognized that what is true of individuals is also true of governments. Whatever the revenue may be, there will always be the pressing need to spend it. But between governments and individuals there is this vital difference, that the government rarely pauses even to consider what its income is. Were any of us to adopt the methods of public finance in our private affairs, we should ignore the total of our income and consider only what we should like to spend. We might decide on a second car, an extension of the home, a motor launch as well as a yacht, a country place and a long holiday in Bermuda. All these, we should tell each other, are essential. It would remain only to adjust our income to cover these bare necessities; and if we economize at all, it will be in matters of taxation. A government by contrast, which applied the methods of individual finance to public expenditure would begin by attempting to estimate what its actual revenue should be. Given so much to spend, how much should be allocated to what? A federal government which decided upon this

novel approach to the subject would be responsible for a revolution in public finance. It is the chief object of this book to suggest that such a revolution, of which we have seen some hint in California, is now generally overdue.

Governmental as opposed to individual income is historically linked with the incidence of war. In all systems of revenue there has always been provision for the temporary expenses of conflict. During a time of emergency, with our interests, our beliefs, our pride or even our existence at stake, we agree to pay almost anything as the price of victory. The war ends and with it the temporary expenses which everyone has seen to be more or less inevitable. In theory the revenue should fall to something like its previous level. In practice it seldom does. While the governmental income remains almost at its wartime level, peacetime expenditure rises to meet it. In times past the action of this law was slightly restrained, to be sure, by two considerations which no longer apply. In the first place, it was usually felt that taxes had to be reduced somewhat in time of peace in order to allow of their being raised again in time of war. During a century, however, when each successive war is judged to be the last, this theory finds no further support. In the second place, there are types of extravagance which yield only a diminishing return. To the provision of banquets and the enjoyment of dancing girls there is (eventually) a physical limit. The same is not true, unfortunately, of departmental and technical luxuriance. Economic and cultural advisers can multiply beyond the point at which concubines might be thought a bore; beyond the point even at which they might be thought unbearable. Financially as well as aesthetically, the situation has become infinitely worse.

In countries like Britain and the United States the initiative in public finance comes from subdepartments of government which decide each year on their needs for the year that is to come. After allowing for present costs and future developments the experienced civil servant adds 10 per cent to the total, assuming (not always correctly) that his bid will be challenged at some stage by the financial branch. Assuming, however, that the expected wrangle takes place, the added 10 per cent is deleted at departmental level when the combined estimate comes to be drawn up. To this estimate the head of the department adds 10 per cent again, assuming (not always correctly) that his bid will be challenged by the Treasury. After the expected dispute, the revised estimate is laid before the responsible Minister, in England the Chancellor of the Exchequer, who consolidates all the departmental demands in a grand total and decides how the revenue can be made to equal the expenditure. With the agreement of his colleagues, he presents the nation with the bill. Here is the sum total of what the government needs, and these are the taxes which the people will have to pay.

But what, it will be asked, of the safeguards? Are not the accounts and estimates laid before the people's representatives? Is there no Treasury Department to act as watchdog over the public purse? Are there no regulations framed to check extravagance and waste? All these safeguards undoubtedly exist. That they are futile is manifest from the known results. The reasons for their futility are less obvious, however, and are perhaps worth investigating, both as curious in themselves and as affording the clue to possible improvement. Briefly, the answer is that the accounts are meaningless, the Treasury ineffective and the regulations so contrived as to make economy not so much difficult as impossible.

To deal first with the accounts and estimates presented to the House of Commons and available to the public, it is interesting to learn that a procedure of Exchequer receipts, dating from about 1129 and involving a Teller, a Tally Cutter, an Auditor, a Clerk of the Pells, a Scriptor Talliar and several Chamberlains, survived until 1826. Apart from this, however, the basic fact to learn is that the accounts, such as they are, were designed for use during one particular period of history. Introduced during the Second Dutch War (in 1666), their primary object was to prevent money from the Navy Vote being spent by Charles II on the aptly entitled Duchess of Portsmouth. Even for this strictly limited purpose the method chosen met with no startling success. The system was revised, therefore, so as to assume its present form in 1689, from which year it more or less prevented William III from spending the money on *his* friends, who were not even girls.

Devised originally to guard the till, the public form of accounting dates from a period before bookkeeping by double entry was generally known except among nonconformists like Defoe. It dates, moreover, from an age when few gentlemen knew even the arabic numerals, the clock face in the stable yard showing only the Roman figures which the classically educated might be expected to understand. The result is that these public accounts, not of the latest pattern even in 1689, are now beginning to verge on the obsolete. They were revised, it is true, as a result of an inquiry held in 1828-29, but the minority report of the professional accountant was set aside in favor of the civil servants' recommendations; these were against double entry and left untouched the previous confusion between liabilities and assets, between capital and current. In 1904 Mr. Thomas Gibson Bowles, M.P., could therefore describe the national accounts as "unsystematic, unscientific, complicated, and so presented as to conceal and even to falsify the facts." In 1957 Mr. John Applebey remarked that those responsible for the public accounts seem to confuse themselves as well as everyone else.

It is fair to conclude, in short, that the British public accounts are not quite in line with current methods of accountancy. As a means of control, as a system of imparting information, they are scarcely worth the paper they are printed on. Accounts which would disgrace and discredit a third-rate dog-racing company are solemnly presented each year to the nation, and often presented by a businessman who ought to and does know better. So far from being improved in form, these accounts have become more complex and muddled as the sums involved have proliferated and swollen. They are not true and they do not balance. It is the business of the accountant to give the facts of the financial position in the language of business, which is money. In that language he is to tell the truth and the whole truth. But those who present accounts to the nation do nothing of the kind. They present only a picture of archaic and dignified confusion.

And what of the Treasury, that guardian of the public weal? The accepted principle is that new expenditure is watched by the Treasury, old expenditure by the departments themselves. But what sort of financial control is this? The division of responsibility is meaningless, for the problem of true economy is one and indivisible. Under such a system the extra clerk is demanded while the surplus clerk is retained. No office is ever declared redundant for fear that it should again be wanted and that its revival would mean a new approach to the Treasury. Nor would the surrender of an established post in Department A make it any easier to establish a different post in Department B, the two problems being considered in fact by separate authorities and as things totally unrelated to each other. Such a practice can lead only to an irresponsible attitude among those forbidden to regard the problem as a whole. And experience suggests that grown men treated as children can behave in a very childish way.

As for the regulations imposed on the official, all they do is to add rigidity to waste. The whole system of appropriations is convenient only for cash accounting and useless for purposes of control. The departmental appropriation does not represent, to begin with, the cost of the department to which it relates. The Army Vote excludes stationery, for that is supplied by H.M. Stationery Office; the Stationery Office Vote excludes buildings (because these belong to the Office of Works) and so it goes on. Nor does the appropriation correspond to what is being done. Thus, the Navy's Votes are serialized from 1 (for pay) to 15 (for additional married quarters), with separate votes for such things as shipbuilding, armaments and the Admiralty Office. Similarly, the Army Account is serialized into Votes: No. 1 for Pay, 7 for Supplies, 9 for Warlike Stores, and so forth. But neither the Navy nor the Army is organized like that. The Navy is organized into units afloat and ashore. The Army is organized in battalions, batteries, depots and schools, for which individually no cost is shown. All that the system ensures is that money voted for vehicles should not be spent on weapons. But what if it were?

And what is the point of the distinction? The Legislature should not concern itself with that. What the faithful lawmakers might more usefully watch is the relative cost of administration and troops. How many extra battalions might be maintained for the sum spent on the finance branch of the War Office? Which are we more likely to need in an emergency — minute sheets or bayonets, ledgers or guns? That is a question of policy whereas the total allocation for uniform clothing is almost solely a matter for the expert. The present rigidity is merely a waste of effort, money and time, serving no useful purpose of any kind.

So much for the official safeguards. In the light of their failure, all that remains to check extravagance is the press and the public. It might be thought that these would be effective, the press having no great love for bureaucracy and the body of taxpayers having a direct interest in the economical handling of their affairs. Why should press and public prove helpless where their own interests are so vitally concerned? The answer to that question is that true economy cannot be imposed on an organization from outside; it must begin at the center. From time to time the press does take up the cry of official extravagance, publishing details of apparent waste which the departments concerned are often in a position to contradict. More often the attacks are simply ignored, the civil servants well knowing that the newspapers will turn to something else in a few days' time. Suppose, however, that the outcry leads to questions in the House and that proof is forthcoming of some of the allegations made, what is the result? The inevitable sequel is the appointment of an investigating committee, a device intended to postpone the business until after the next election. The official inquiry begins its laborious work, the members of the committee being (let us assume) experienced, intelligent, energetic and ruthless. They achieve little or nothing. Why? Because the whole process is basically wrong.

Let us suppose that naval dockyards are the subject of inquiry and that the investigators descend upon each in turn. The members include retired admirals and practicing engineers who are far from ignorant of the matter in hand. They hear evidence. They ask searching questions: "What are these fellows supposed to be doing?" "What is all this junk?" "How do you dispose of the clinker and wood shavings?" "Why pay so many people to do so little?" But they soon observe a phenomenon which is best explained in terms of zoology. In the presence of wolves, sheep are said to form a tight bunch with horns outward and the weakest in the center. Civil servants do the same. Faced by a common danger, they take up that formation, yielding nothing, denying everything, concealing all. This is a well-known fact of biology and one against which the committee members must struggle in vain. Their report, when eventually printed, might just as well be placed in the toilet. Whatever happens to it, the matter is allowed to drop.

The ordinary taxpayer is often in a better position to know about waste in administration than either the politician or the journalist. For one thing, he may himself be employed in the dockyard. It is theoretically his interest as well as his duty to come forward and denounce extravagance when he sees it. He does nothing of the kind, and that for two distinct reasons. In the first place he stands to gain nothing but unpopularity and abuse, being likely to be regarded as at best a crank, at worst a spy. In the second place, he knows perfectly well that the money saved in one direction will certainly be wasted in another. Nothing he can do will reduce the tax he has to pay. So he wisely decides to say nothing and keep the good opinion of his neighbors. In matters of public expenditure no help is to be expected from the public at large unless the informant is personally rewarded and at the same time assured that all savings made will go to the reduction of the taxes to which he is subject.

To summarize the position, the public revenue is regarded as limitless and expenditure rises eternally to meet it, and the various devices which are supposed to check expenditure fail to do so, being wrongly conceived and imperfectly motivated. The problem is a serious one and would seem to merit our attention. What is to be done? The modern instinct is to frame new regulations and laws, of which there are already more than enough. The better plan, less fashionable today, is to remotivate the people actually concerned, penalizing the extravagance we now reward and rewarding the economy we now penalize. As a first step toward redirecting the flood, we need to reverse the whole process of government finance. Ministers should not begin by ascertaining what the departments need. They should begin by asking what the country can afford to spend. We do not base our personal budget on what our past extravagances have taught us to like but on the income we can fairly expect to receive. We do not, in short, plan to spend what we have not got. The same principle should apply to public as it does to individual finance. The first question to decide is the ratio between the revenue and the gross national product. What propor-

tion of the national income should the government demand? What proportion of the individual's income can the government safely take? And what happens when that proportion is exceeded? Economists (with one notable exception) have fought shy of this problem, allowing it to be assumed that, where government expenditure is concerned, the sky is the limit. It is one aim of this book to suggest that there are other and lower limits; a limit beyond which taxation is undesirable, a limit beyond which it is dangerous and a limit (finally) beyond which it is fatal. And these limits are clearly indicated by both economic theory and historical fact.

In the light of these known dangers, it is for the Cabinet to decide upon the ratio between government expenditure and gross national product. That decision taken, there is a total fixed for the revenue, a total within which the Ministries have to work. It is for the Cabinet again to decide upon the distribution of this total between the departments. To individual departmental heads would fall the responsibility of subdividing departmental allocations between the various branches and units. No department under this system would be asked to submit an estimate. It would be told, instead, to keep within a total. All that would concern the Legislature would be the gross expenditure and its allocation to Departments. Lawmakers need not be asked to vote on the relative amounts to be spent on gasoline and grease, floor polish and boots. They *can* fairly compare the value for money given by the Air Force or the British Council, by Education or by Health. For purposes of control, they need no more than that by way of forecast, together with *real* accounts of expenditure in the past — such accounts as they have never yet been allowed to see.

The obvious advantage of the system here described is that a limit is placed on expenditure. An advantage as important, if less obvious, is that the expenditure becomes flexible within each Ministry, Department, subdepartment and unit. The officials themselves are thus made responsible for economy, their success or failure becoming instantly apparent from the accounts of the following year. It is the executive officers, and they alone, who know where economies can safely be made. Once they understand that the development they want in one direction is conditional on their economizing in another direction, the rest can safely be left to them; provided that promotion goes first to the man who shows where the money can be saved. Yet another advantage, still less obvious at first sight, would be the elimination of Treasury supervision with all its evils of divided control, inefficiency and waste. In place of distrustful interference, the public official would know only the strong leash of account and audit. He would be compelled to accept responsibility, free to display initiative and forced to recognize that cost and value are but different aspects of the same idea.

Once the decision has been made to approach the financial problem from the right direction, it would remain only to enlist public aid in the prevention of waste. For this purpose the first need is for an independent tribunal to which all proposals for saving money could be submitted; a body of, say, three, to include a government representative. This tribunal would hear representations from the public and from the departments affected and would decide finally whether each suggested economy were feasible or not. Each decision in favor of an economy would lead to an executive order to the department concerned, reducing its future allocation by the amount to be saved. It would be the further function of the tribunal to reward each successful applicant by the remission of his income tax proportionally to the amount of the saving. There should also be provision to ensure that all sums saved should go, not to another department, nor to the Treasury, but solely to the reduction of the National Debt. The last function of the tribunal would be to recommend for the highest honors the citizens whose suggestions had resulted in the greatest economies, as also the civil servants who had been most successful in reducing needless expenditure. A minor revolution would date from the day when officials came to realize that reputation is more readily to be won by saving money than by spending it.

It is not to be supposed that the reform of the national finances would be unopposed. In this field of administration the reformer will be faced, inevitably, by a closed phalanx of civil servants representing one of the strongest vested interests in the world. Their opposition, though passive, will be formidable. To all proposals for a proper system of accounts they will reply with a pitying smile that it was tried once at the War Office, found wasteful and long ago abandoned. They will then retire behind a smoke screen of technical mysteries, muttering finally that public finance is a more complex matter than is generally realized. Figures cannot lie but liars can figure.

The hieratic and esoteric attitudes observable in the British Treasury have led to the creation of a special term to describe the cult: esoterrorism. In the eighteenth century these same esoterrorists concealed the mysteries of the Exchequer in medieval Latin and in the court hand which the law courts abandoned in 1733, continuing indeed to do so until the Exchequer itself (but not its Chancellor) was abolished in the reign of William IV. Nor was the Exchequer alone in its archaic confusion, for an investigation of 1570 into the London Customs broke down completely because "the officers have used such an obscure way in the keeping of their books." A Member of Parliament exclaimed in 1691, "I stand amazed that in the best times and Governments, things should be in such darkness." The special commissioners of 1829 reported that "The Annual Accounts leave millions unexplained and unaccounted for in detail" — which was found again to be the case in 1844 and is still so today. The darkness has become, if anything, darker still, for to the original confusion of the accounts has been added the babble of consultants and the jargon of the London School of Economics. From being merely a nuisance, esoterrorism is fast becoming a religion.

The strongholds of esoterrorism have been impregnable since the days of Gladstone. Amid the entanglements which surround their position are the graves of their former assailants, Florence Nightingale, Sir John Keane and Lord Randolph Churchill. There too is the mutilated tombstone of Sir Charles Harris, the man who nearly betrayed the whole position, on the anniversary of whose death the leading esoterrorists still exchange a barbed wire. Let no one imagine that this citadel will yield to the first assault. Let no one doubt, however, that it will yield to the last.

2

ANCIENT AND MODERN

AND IT came to pass in those days that there went out a decree from Caesar Augustus, that all the world should be taxed. This decree seems to have been enforced ever since. It is only fair, however, to add that Augustus was not actually the first ruler to whom this idea had occurred. Taxation is as old as time and takes its earliest form in the action of the petty chief who builds himself a stockade at the estuary, the river junction or mountain pass and levies a toll on the passing traveler or merchant. This has always been the easiest tax to collect, being described as a charitable subscription, customs duty or blackmail, all according to the point of view. It is seldom worth the merchant's while to fight his way past the barricade because the amount of this exaction can be charged to the eventual purchaser of the goods, the merchant knowing that rival traders will have to do the same. The sum demanded, in varying tones of appeal or menace, is roughly equivalent

to the additional expense involved in going round by another and less frequented route, and is exorbitant only when no such route exists. The cost of the tax is much the same, in short, as the cost of avoidance.

Next in antiquity is the tax on land, which is at least relatively easy to collect. This is akin to protection money paid to the gangster, the basic idea of feudalism. The cultivator of land is vulnerable to the extent that his whereabouts are known and the extent of his property defined. He cannot disclaim ownership without losing it, so that he will pay for the recognition of his boundaries and the exclusion of other people's cattle. The amount he will pay is roughly equivalent to the cost of moving to another area beyond the gangster's reach, and becomes exorbitant only when no such place can be found. A variant of the tax on land is the tax on produce, which represents greater difficulties of assessment. Historically, the latest development of this is the tax on income, which becomes technically possible only in an urban civilization from which subsistence farming has almost disappeared and in which the people are law-abiding and literate. The collection of this tax is extremely complex but it has so far been supposed to have no limit other than the cost of moving elsewhere — which, for many of the victims, may be impracticable. We shall see, however, in a later chapter what its effective limits are.

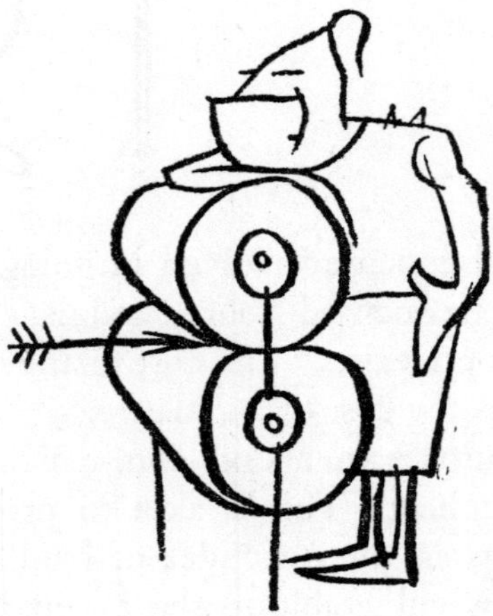

In studying the history of taxation we soon come to realize that taxes fall into two broad categories; those that people impose on themselves and those they inflict upon others. Some effort is made to keep the former to the minimum consistent with the objects in view. There is nothing, by contrast, to prevent the latter reaching (and often exceeding) the limit of the victims' willingness to pay. With either category we have seen that the level of taxation rises in time of war without falling to the same extent in time of peace. Taxes tend to increase, therefore, according to the law which governs their growth, becoming heavier until the point is reached at which society collapses under their weight. We shall see that this has often happened in the past and may presumably happen again; sooner, indeed, than is generally realized.

Among the earliest systems of taxation of which we have detailed knowledge is that of the Chaldees, among whom a tax of 10 per cent on produce was usual but often exceeded in practice. Of Darius, King of Persia, it has been calculated that his money revenue amounted to £28,000,000 (around $133,000,000) in the values of 1904, additional tribute being received by him in kind, surtax being payable in eunuchs. We do not know, unfortunately, what proportion this would be of the national produce, nor indeed of the individual's wealth, but that it fell short of 10 per cent in either case seems fairly clear.

It would be a grave mistake to publish a learned work in which there was no reference to Nineveh.[1] And it so happens that documents found there do shed some light on the problems of tax collection. A harassed official wrote some letters to Tiglath Pileser III (745–727 B.C.) describing his difficulties in collecting the taxes at Tyre and Sidon. The duties were levied on wine, as also on the timber of Lebanon, but reluctance to pay took the form of killing

[1] Nineveh, capital of the Assyrian empire, is among the earliest cities to have encountered the traffic problem. The place contained, according to the prophet Jonah, "more than six score thousand persons, that cannot discern between their right hand and their left" (Jonah 4:11). The confusion can be imagined and was evidently notorious. The solution was to turn the ramparts (100 feet in height) into a one-direction three-lane skyway for the faster vehicles. How this was done is described by Diodorus (S.2, 3).

one tax collector at Tyre, his colleague at Sidon being rescued with difficulty by the police.

It is also usual in works of learning to refer, sooner or later, to ancient Athens. This book will be no exception, difficult as it is to maintain for long the reverent attitude associated with classical scholarship. The Athens admired in the classical VI Form is, of course, purely imaginary, the invention of classical philologists in whom any sense of history (or of reality) is almost completely lacking. It is well, however, to bring it in occasionally, thus lending tone to the whole book and hinting that the author went to the right sort of school (as in fact he did). Now, Athens[2] provides an early example of what is called democracy. This did not mean that the Athenian revenue came solely from the taxes which the people of Athens had agreed to pay. On the contrary, Athenian revenue consisted largely of sums collected in blackmail from other parts of Greece. Archaeological evidence is plentiful on this subject. From inscriptions of the period of the Archidamian War we know that payments were made at the time of the Dyonysiac festival, received by the Apodektai, who paid the money to the Hellenotamiai. One of these inscriptions is supposed to make the procedure tolerably clear.

Coming to a later period, we must next study the Revenue Laws of Ptolemy Philadelphus, who ruled Egypt

[2] Athens became an example of democratic government at some period in the middle of the nineteenth century when that form of rule was becoming fashionable in Britain and the United States. Athenian democracy is thus mentioned in only one line of Lemprière's *Classical Dictionary* or *Bibliotheca Classica*, re-edited by E. H. Barker from the seventh American edition prepared by Charles Anthon, Adjunct Professor of Languages and Ancient Geography in Columbia College (wherever that may be), New York. London, 1838.

from about 284 to 246 B.C. The Revenue Papyrus, discovered by Professor Flinders Petrie in 1893-94, is our authority for the methods of tax collection used in Ptolemaic Egypt. From this we learn the essential fact that the taxes laid upon vineyards, orchards and oil amounted to one-sixth (or nearly 17 per cent) of the produce and no more. We also hear that the chief tax farmer, holding a two-year contract for the tax on oil, commencing from the month Gorpizeus (or Mesore in the Egyptian Calendar with which the reader may be more familiar) might receive no payment except in the presence of the oeconomicus and antigrapheus and had to report in triplicate to the dioecetes and eclogistes. From all this it will be realized that methods of taxation were highly developed in the ancient world. We gain the same impression from a study of Syria under the Seleucids. But there too the rate of taxation was not exorbitant, being in fact no more than 7 per cent of the total product.

Turning to other and later societies we must make at least some passing reference to taxation in the Roman, Indian and Chinese Empires. Of Roman taxation all too little has been discovered. In the time of Augustus, Roman citizens are known to have paid a 5 per cent tax on the inheritance of estates. They also paid municipal taxes, of which we have no exact record, and customs duties at each provincial frontier, which are not supposed to have been onerous. Their subject peoples were less fortunate but we hardly know to what extent. At the time of the Empire's collapse, the taxation of the provinces seems to have been crushing — too heavy, in fact, to be effective — and historians have agreed in regarding this as a principal cause of the disaster. Almost all that can be said with certainty about taxation under the later emperors is that it lacked any sort of continuity, consisting of urgent, exorbitant and frequent demands arising from particular crises. Its effect was so to discourage production that landowners and cultivators fled from the land and took refuge where they could, letting their fields go out of cultivation.

The history of ancient India reveals a sharp contrast between the Hindu and Moslem concepts of imperial finance. The Laws of Manu define what the Hindu king's taxes were supposed to be. They rise to no more than a sixth part of certain classes of produce, with an eighth, a twelfth or a fiftieth on others. Under the Muslim emperors of the Mogul Dynasty, on the other hand, the theory was upheld that all land belonged to the monarch, that a life tenure was the most that was possible for the subject, and that even this was terminable at the sovereign's pleasure. With land thus reverting to the crown at the landholder's death, no concept of true ownership could arise. This is an instance of death duties amounting to 100 per cent. As regards taxation, Muslim law gave the king one-fifth of the gross produce but the Moguls actually took one-third. From the Hindus, moreover, they were known to take as much as half. Their fiscal policy fluctuated but its final effect was disastrous. Large tracts of land went out of cultivation, trade declined, and it was the collapse of Mogul rule which prepared the way for British intervention after 1707.

There was no equivalent collapse in China. There, taxation under the Tsing Dynasty (1644-1911) has been made the subject of a book by Mr. Shao Kuan Chew. The Chinese land tax was established, it seems, in A.D. 770, revenue being later derived also from a poll tax (based on land), customs duties, and a special tax to maintain the postal service.

Taxes may at times have amounted to as much as 20 per cent of the national income. But this was contrary to the accepted ideas of Confucius, who was himself a tax collector at one stage of his official career and found (to his dismay) that the Dukes of Lu, in whose service he was, had doubled the taxes by increasing the proportion from one-tenth to one-fifth of the produce. In the words of his biographer:

> . . . It was assumed that one-tenth of the produce should be ample to meet all governmental expenses . . . The original provision for the collection of one-tenth of the produce had been established by one of the early Kings of the Golden Age of the country, and was generally accepted as a perfectly just and equitable system of taxation; any departure from it was resented as an injustice.

Such injustices were not unknown, but, in theory at least, the burden of Chinese taxes would not seem to have been excessive.

Coming to the history of the modern nations, we find that the first three to aim at ascendancy on the imperial scale were Spain, the Netherlands and France. As each failed in turn, excessive taxation played a part in its decline. From the Spanish example no clear lesson can be drawn, for while Philip II was the founder of modern bureaucratic practice, his tax system was not the most significant feature of his rule. His two chief indirect taxes were the alcabala and the millones, the former a 10 per cent purchase tax, and the latter a tax on oil, wine and vinegar. Other taxes affected salt, tobacco and playing cards. Despite these efforts to increase the revenue, the Spanish government was virtually bankrupt by 1693, but taxes were only in part the cause of ruin. The country was undermined as much by its nationalized industries as by its taxation, and as much again perhaps by its religious intolerance. Where Spanish taxes feature most prominently in the history books is when they were applied to the Netherlands by the Duke of Alva. What was proposed at one stage was a levy of 1/100 part of all property, a tax of 1/20 on the sale of real estate and a tax of 1/10 on the sale of merchandise.

> It was evident that a tax of a tenth on sales would deal a mortal blow to commerce . . . The king's partisans were the first to try to turn the governor from a measure as imprudent as it was impracticable . . . (Motley)

So much for purchase tax. The commerce of the Netherlands was to be affected by many things, of which taxation was only one.

As an aggressively imperial power, Spain was succeeded by the Dutch Republic, that part of the Netherlands which was under the leadership of Holland. During the brief period of Dutch ascendancy there were great difficulties over finance. Taxes were levied, as we know, on corn, on flour, on bread and on fish, becoming ruinous after 1672. There were anti-taxation riots in 1678 and Renier writes of the War of the Spanish Succession that "during the war the Dutch Republic bled itself white." But the taxation remained even after the peace, Dutch capital being increasingly invested in the French and British Funds. In 1751 a group of prominent merchants submitted to the Stadtholder, William IV, a paper on the state of trade in which they stated that its decline was largely the result of oppressive taxes. What they advised was "an attempt to discountenance and prevent pilfering, waste, sluttishness, neglects, extravagance in housekeeping, with other indiscretions and bad management," and some such attempt did actually result. A campaign against waste, sluttishness, neglect and extravagance would not be out of place in other countries at a later period of their history.

A last example of fatal taxation is to be found in the history of France. Every schoolboy has been compelled at some stage of his life to memorize the causes of the French Revolution. Some part of what he commits to memory is approximately correct, and he fills in the background with vivid if slightly contradictory impressions derived respectively from Dickens and Baroness Orczy. He ends with the conviction that taxation had something to do with it, and so indeed it had. His difficulty lies in attempting to discover what the taxes actually amounted to; a difficulty

which historians seem to share. To gain any sort of picture of the situation, we have somehow to disentangle the references to taxes, both central and provincial, from the references to manorial dues, which corresponded to rent. Readers unduly shocked by these relics of feudalism should note that they survived in England until abolished by an Act of 1935, which did not fully take effect for another decade; manorial royalties on mineral deposits being payable until the year when the mines were nationalized. French feudal dues (like their English equivalent) have also to be distinguished from parish tithes, which in France seem to have varied between 1/12 and 1/20 of certain crops, many others being exempt. If manorial dues and tithes are regarded, respectively, as rent and local tax, the royal taxation comprised the greater part of what still remained to pay. It included the *taille*, the capitation, the *dixième*, and a number of indirect taxes of which the gabelle, or salt tax, has attracted the most attention. The *taille* was the feudal levy raised from those of the population who performed no military service; the nobles, clergy and most office-holders being exempt. The capitation of 1695 and the *dixième* of 1710 were both intended to fall on everybody, and both ended merely as an addition to the *taille*. What then did the *taille* amount to? It seems to have varied considerably both from year to year and from place to place, but may have represented something between 33 and 36 per cent of the taxpayer's income. Taxes and tithe may have taken from 38 to 41 per cent between them.

As an example to finance ministers of the present day the *Ancien Régime* is important in two respects. It shows, first of all, the ultimate limits of taxation; the point of refusal which becomes the moment for revolt. It shows,

Osborn

in the second place, the danger of treating capital as income. On the first point, much has been made of the peasants' hardships, all in subsequent justification of a revolution which had already taken place. The fact seems to be, however, that the peasants were more prosperous than they had been for centuries, only they were adept at concealing such wealth as they may have had. What is significant is not the traditional farmer's tale of woe but the fact, then universally recognized, that no further tax would bring in any more money. At a certain point, probably short of 45 per cent, the expenses of collection would have exceeded the value of the sum collected. Short of that again was the point of rebellion. All this suggests that there is a limit beyond which taxation cannot be made to go.

The reader may object that the real trouble about the French taxation was that it fell only on those relatively poor. In so far as this is true, it goes to illustrate our second point. What the French government had done was to meet present needs by mortgaging its future revenue. The majority of those who were exempt from direct taxation had purchased their exemption by a capital sum. Cities like Bordeaux and Grenoble had commuted the tax in this way. Most of the noble families had purchased their patents of nobility and hence their immunity by payment of a lump sum during some previous reign. Office holders were mostly exempt from taxation but these again had bought their offices for a price which was enhanced by this very consideration. It is inexact to say that the French upper classes were exempt from taxation as a matter of inherited privilege. All but the most ancient nobility had been allowed to commute the tax by payment in advance.

The upper classes of today, whether in Britain or the

United States, have been less fortunate. It is a question, however, whether modern governments have been much more provident. The collection of death duties has much the same effect, in anticipating future income, as the sale of nobility. The heir to the estate receives nothing, it is true, for his capital payment, but the state has equally mortgaged its future income. The outward trappings of privilege may be missing (and these were at least picturesque) but the financial mistake is the same: the error of confusing capital with income. When we study the fate of the Old Regime in France, we shall do well to pass lightly over the details of oppression and concentrate on the central fact. The Old Regime did not collapse because it was tyrannical or cruel, nor even because it was obsolete. It collapsed because it was bankrupt.

3

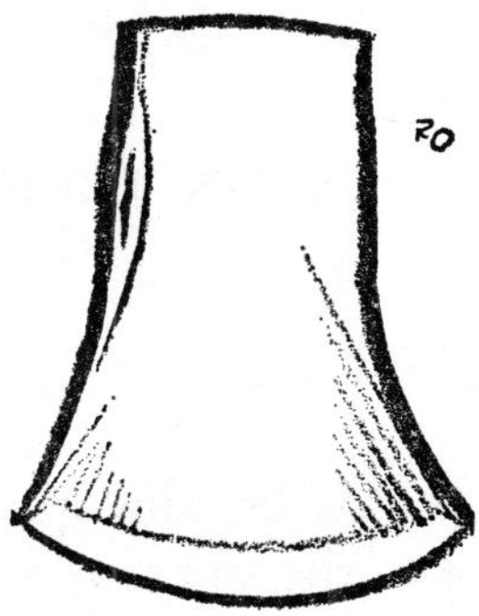

THE TAX ON INCOME

THE STORY of taxation is, broadly speaking, the story of war; and, increasingly, the story of war taxes being retained after the war is over. Of all war taxes, that on income is the most significant. It was first introduced in Britain, amending a system of direct taxation which had its origin in 1692. The English revenue of the previous year, 1691, amounted to £4,501,107. 19s. 8½d., the halfpenny turning out to be an error but on the credit side. Direct taxation began in the following year with a land tax and assessed taxes on menservants, horses, carriages and windows. The tax on income began with an Act passed by the British House of Commons on January 9, 1799. It was not unopposed, the Common Council of the City of London holding that "to tax the precarious and fluctuating income arising from the labour and industry of Persons in Trade, Professions, etc. . . . is most partial, cruel and oppressive." The inquisitorial methods involved were widely regarded as "inconsistent with the principles of the British Constitution and repugnant to the feelings of Englishmen." Be that as it may, the Act became law, imposing a tax of 10 per cent on all incomes over £200 a year with a reduced rate on incomes under £200 but over £60 and exemption of incomes below that figure. The yield was disappointing, the tax being fairly easy to evade, and Pitt's successor, Addington, replaced it in 1803 with an income tax of almost the present outward form, complete with deduction at the source and Schedules A, B, C and D. Sir Francis Burdett reminded the House of Commons in 1804 that "a little before the introduction of this unprincipled scheme of plunder," the law of perjury (applicable to taxpayers who made a false return) was amended so as to make the offense punishable by transportation to Botany Bay. Fixed originally at 1s. in the £, income tax rose during the Napoleonic Wars to 1s.3d. and finally to 2s. in 1806; a level which the second Marquis of Lansdowne regarded, interestingly, as its "natural limit." A tax on hawkers, peddlers, and petty bagmen reached its natural limits even sooner, a revenue of £9289. 16s. 3¾d. costing no less than £2786. 3s. 9d. to collect.

It would be no exaggeration to say that this first income tax was unpopular. Acceptable only as a means of defeating Napoleon, it was widely regarded as unconstitutional and oppressive, the *Edinburgh Review* observing that "we cannot suppose that a free people will endure it for one instant after the crisis has passed." Nor did they, the tax being abolished in 1815. The shuddering legislators expressed their loathing by the further decree that all documents and returns should be destroyed (which actually they were not, or at least not entirely). A heavy indirect taxation, also of Addington's devising, remained as a discouragement to industry. It was well exemplified in the notorious PARKINSON'S CASE of 1824, an instance of the oppressions which had by then become customary but one almost entirely overlooked by students of constitutional history. Mr. Peter Parkinson, who lived (it will be remembered) at Flashby-with-Winterburn in Yorkshire, was most unjustly assessed in respect of two horses and a groom, whereas the second horse was merely being broken in, for sale. When the appellant's case was very properly upheld by the Commissioners, the surveyor appealed to the judges on circuit, who reversed the Commissioners' decision; an injustice for which all legal history scarcely affords a parallel.

Such was the weight of this indirect taxation that William Cobbett, in 1829, advised all tradesmen, farmers and even gentlemen to emigrate to America as their sole means of escape from ruin. The taxes, he pointed out, together with poor rates, county and parish rates, came to "twice as much as the rent of all real property in the kingdom." He emphasized that "what a man pays in taxes is just as much of *loss* to him and of loss for ever, exactly as much so as if it were tossed into the sea." He brought his argument to its climax in a passage which deserves quotation in full.

> . . . If we ride in a chaise, or a coach, or on a horse: if we keep a dog; if we have a window to see through, a servant to assist us, a large part of the cost is tax. We can have no title to property, no right of occupation; we can neither lend nor borrow, nor pay nor receive money; nor can we ask for law or justice without paying a tax; and when the breath is out of our bodies, the government demands a strict account of our bequests, and takes from our children or others, a large part of what we leave behind . . .

Cobbett's advice to emigrate is tersely summarized in the admirable dictum which events so often justify: "Some people have a notion, that, when things come to their worst, they will mend. Why should they?"

Why indeed? One proposal for amending them, put forward anonymously in 1831, was for a capital levy of 20 per cent which would pay off the national debt and leave the country untaxed "excepting the small proportion sufficient to support the government." Nothing so drastic was attempted and the drifting and muddled expenses of a reformed Parliament tended rather to increase. Such was the position when Sir Robert Peel assumed office in 1841. It was he who reintroduced the income tax in his budget of the following year.

In general, as we have seen, the pattern has been for taxation to be imposed in time of war and then retained in time of peace. To this rule, Peel's action of 1842 would seem, at first sight, to be the chief exception. This view is, however, mistaken, and that for three reasons. In the first place, Peel had on his hands the Canadian rebellion of 1838-43, which cost £2,096,046, and also the First China War of 1840-43, which cost £2,201,028; nor was Peel to know that these admittedly minor campaigns might not last longer and cost more. In the second place, Peel was closely associated with the Duke of Wellington, who was always ready for a new war with France; a war which seemed at times quite probable, and the approach of which appeared to justify some costly efforts in fortification. Last of all, the new tax was to replace, not merely supplement, the existing taxes on expenditure (or many of them), being planned "to revive commerce" and to last, at 7d. in the pound, for no more than four years. It is scarcely necessary to add that this was a proportional tax, payable at the same rate on all incomes over a certain level.

War, when it came, was with Russia, not with France; the result, it was afterwards felt, of backing the wrong horse. The effect of the war was to raise the basic rate in

1854 from 7d. to 1s.4d., doubling the yield and at the same time making permanent what had hitherto been regarded as temporary. The Crimean War actually cost £69,277,-694, no inconsiderable sum. It was Gladstone who was in office at the time and no one could have deplored the situation more than did he. For their money the taxpayers had, among other things, the Charge of the Light Brigade and the invention of the cardigan. But the tax went on when the war ended, value for money being now conspicuously absent. And it was Gladstone himself who perceived that the expenditure was the result of the tax. He made this clear in his speech to the House of Commons on May 13, 1858:

> I believe that it [the income tax] does more than any other tax to demoralise and corrupt the people . . . So long as you consent, without a special purpose, to levy the income tax as a part of the ordinary and permanent revenue of the country, so long it will be vain to talk of economy and effective reduction of expenditure.

This was especially true because, of the public that might tacitly approve the tax, only a minority had to pay it. Out of a population of 23,325,305 in the Greater Britain of 1861 there were only 278,723 payers of income tax, Schedule D, and a seventh of the total yield came from a mere 4635 taxpayers with incomes of over £2000 a year. Governmental extravagance was being encouraged by the irresponsibility of those who paid little or nothing toward it. By 1866 Gladstone was bewailing the expenditure on public works, pointing out that "vacillation, uncertainty, costliness, extravagance, meanness and all the conflicting vices that could be enumerated, are united in our present system." They still are, but we have ceased to expect anything different.

From the first moment of the income tax's revival the intellectual effort which might have gone toward limiting public expenditure was directed more toward minimizing the individual's contribution. A tax consultant's bill as early as 1852 ran "To enable you to evade the income tax payment, a laborious and intricate work, your account extending over a period of fifteen months, £6.6.0. . . ." One method used was to claim in respect of "an annuity payable to a relation not existing." Another was to divide farms so as to avoid the tenant's tax. As for the tax on personal property, that could be avoided by making deeds of gift. Revenue officials concluded sadly that "it is impossible to prevent these frauds and evasions" and that "the longer the tax continues the more acquainted and instructed people will get how to evade it." John Stuart Mill ended by describing Schedule D as "not a tax on income so much as a tax on conscience." Not all the dishonesty was on the taxpayers' side, incidentally, for large sums were embezzled by the tax collectors themselves, no less than thirty-nine of these defaulting during the three years 1848-50. The evils of income tax began to diminish, however, as the burden was lightened, and in 1874-76 that great man, Sir Stafford Northcote, reduced the standard rate to 2d. in the pound. For a moment it looked as if the tax might disappear, but the moment passed and by 1887 the tax was back at 7d., by 1895 at 8d., and by 1900 it stood at 1s. In 1907, Mr. Asquith openly announced his intention of treating the income tax "as a permanent part of our fiscal machinery." The income tax had indeed come to stay.

Parallel to the story of taxation in Britain is the story of taxation in the United States. Nor are the two stories altogether distinct, for it was an attempt to extend British taxes to the Colonies that brought about the American revolt. The stamp duty which the colonists refused to pay has been paid ever since in Britain by all who sign checks or give receipts for payments. The tea duty to which the Yankees objected is paid to this day in Britain; whereas the American preference for coffee would seem to date from the day when much of their tea supply found its way into Boston harbor. Since American independence had its origin in this refusal to pay taxes imposed by Britain, it is not surprising that the founders of the Union should have had strong views on the subject. These views came to be embodied in the Constitution and specifically in these words:

Article 1. Section 2.

Representatives and direct taxes shall be apportioned among the several States which may be included within this Union, according to their respective numbers.

Article 1. Section 8.

The Congress shall have power to lay and collect taxes, duties, imposts and excises, to pay the debts and pay for the common defense and general welfare of the United States; but all duties, imposts and excises shall be uniform throughout the United States.

Article 1. Section 9.

No capitation or other direct tax shall be laid, unless in proportion to the Census or Enumeration hereinbefore directed to be taken.

To question the wisdom of those who framed the Constitution of the United States would be sacrilege. It might be wished, however, that their wisdom, in this instance, had been more explicit. From these sections of Article 1 it would be natural to infer that direct taxes might be imposed by Congress but were not necessarily to be uniform throughout the United States, although proportionate to the population as ascertained by census. There are those who have sought to justify the further inference that an income tax (proportionate to wealth rather than to numbers) was thus deliberately ruled out. But this is to claim more for the authors than they would ever have claimed for themselves. Never having heard of an income tax, they can scarcely have been at such pains to declare it illegal. What they did know about was the evil of taxation without representation, and this they clearly sought to prevent. That they foresaw the evil of representation without taxation has still perhaps to be proved. It is not unreasonable to conclude that a capitation tax, a tax paid equally by all, was what they had in mind. But it is no less reasonable to deny that this is what they said. Their wisdom is clothed in ambiguity and there is cause to regret that they could not agree more precisely on what they meant. When the federal government ran short of funds during the War between the States, it was not to their own Constitution that the American leaders looked for guidance but to the example of Britain. The result was the beginning of American income tax.

It began with the Act of Congress of August 5, 1861, which imposed a 3 per cent federal income tax. This was superseded almost at once by an Act of March, 1862, signed in July, which, while maintaining a 3 per cent tax on incomes below $10,000, increased the rate to 5 per cent on incomes above that level. This tax was levied in 1863, increased in 1864 and not abolished until 1872. Its legality was upheld by the Supreme Court, which on this subject was later to change its mind. During the five years from 1861 to 1866 the federal expenditure, apart from interest charges, rose to an average of $712,720,000 a year: an increase of 920 per cent on the average of the previous decade. This might not have been serious in itself but (as always) expenditure failed to revert to the previous level. As Mr. F. C. Howe observed in 1896, "the apparent acquiescence of the people in governmental extravagance induced a prodigality in the disposition of public funds which has gone on unabated to the present day." While expenditure fell from its wartime height, it settled at a level representing a 240 per cent increase on prewar expenditure.

Apart from this immediate effect, and apart from the legal issue, the importance of the Act of 1862 lies in its differentiated incidence. In this Act we see the beginning of disproportional or progressive taxation, unknown at that time in Britain. Until that date the Congressman who voted for a tax did so in the knowledge that it would fall as heavily on himself as upon others — a safeguard some might think important — but that principle went in 1862. The significance of this was emphasized at about this time by the economist Mr. J. R. McCulloch. Tax graduation, he said, was not an evil to be paltered with.

> The savages described by Montesquieu who, to get at the fruit cut down the tree, are about as good financiers as the advocates of this sort of taxes. Wherever they are introduced security is necessarily at an end. Even if taxes on income were otherwise the most unexceptional, the adoption of the principle of graduation would make them among the very worst that could be devised. The moment

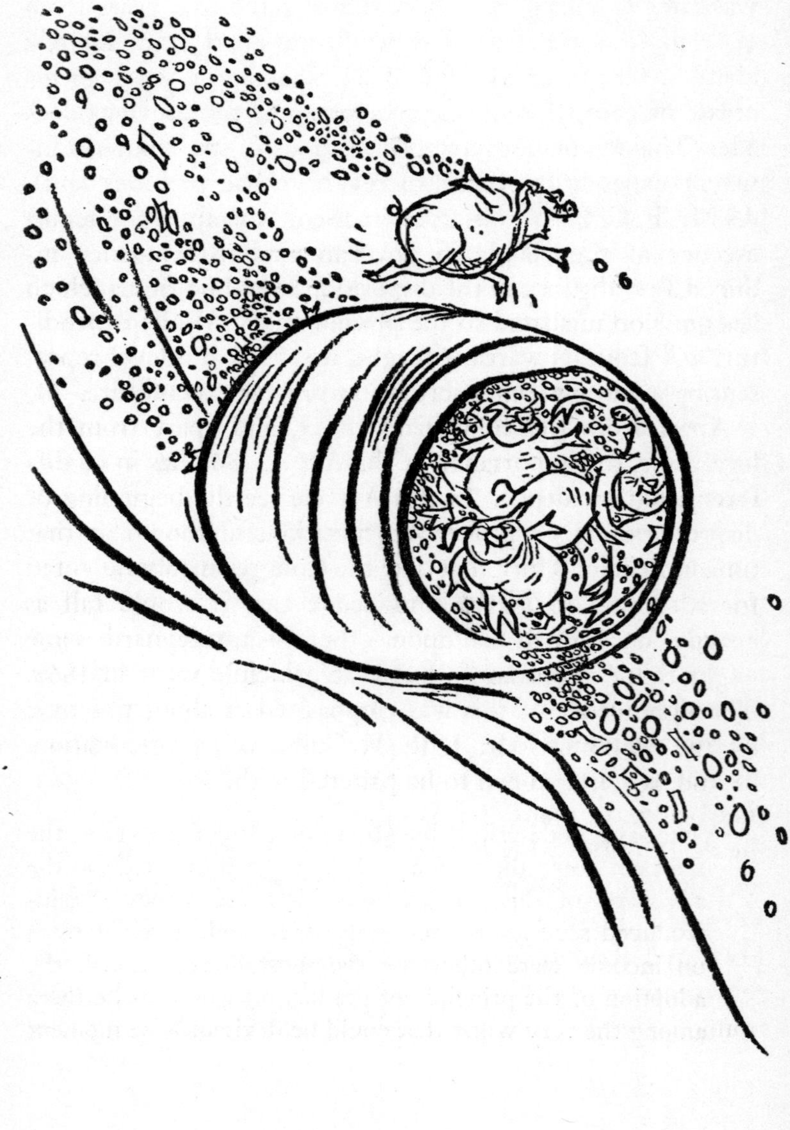

> you abandon, in the framing of such taxes, the cardinal principle of exacting from all individuals the same proportion of their income or their property, you are at sea without rudder or compass, and there is no amount of injustice and folly you may not commit.

The British, in their turn, paid more heed to American example than to McCulloch's warning. Having already introduced death duties some years before, the British placed these on a sliding scale in 1894, varying the rate of 1 per cent on small fortunes to 8 per cent on the greatest. Not only was there no stated principle on which the percentage might be graded but a basic principle was infringed by the confusion of capital with income. Had the yield from death duties been used to reduce the national debt there would have been an element of stability in the situation; but this levy on capital was used from the first for current expenditure.

Oddly enough, the year in which Britain took a further step toward "injustice and folly" was also the year in which the same tendency was resisted, momentarily, in the United States. When an attempt was made to reintroduce income tax there on August 27, 1894, not graduated but fixed at 2 per cent on all incomes over $4000, the tax was ruled out by the Supreme Court as unconstitutional, being a direct tax not proportionate to numbers of population. For the time being, the matter was dropped. In Britain, by contrast, the death duties were being collected, there being no written constitution under which they could be declared illegal. Writing on British Tax-Payers' Rights in 1898, Mr. H. Lloyd Reid referred to death duties as a "class of tax representing probably every form of injustice and uneconomic, arbitrary, and troublesome method possible in taxation." So indeed they are but the Boer War revealed one form of tax incidence which may not even have been foreseen. There was no exemption in favor of those killed in action. The state was thus waiting, vulturelike, to snatch the property of those who had died in its defense. The result was that families in which several were killed might suffer repeated confiscation as well as repeated bereavement. All this, however, was but a foretaste of things to come. The current of public expenditure was quickening as the century came to its close, but the rapids, the quicksands and the rocks lay still some little way ahead.

4

THE TURNING POINT

In the history of taxation the key date, for the English-speaking world, is the year 1909. Until that date the pressure to spend had been mounting in Britain and the United States but the introduction of disproportional taxes had scarcely begun. In so far as they had begun, moreover, the idea was merely that the wealthier citizen should contribute relatively more to government revenue raised for a common purpose, that purpose defined in the American Constitution as provision "for the common defense and general welfare." The danger of disproportional taxes was already apparent in that they could be voted by those who would not have to pay them and on a scale to which there was no defined limit. But so far the general welfare remained the object. All this was changed in 1909, simultaneously, as it happened, in Great Britain and the United States. How this came about is worthy of special attention and careful record.

Regarding Great Britain certainly, and perhaps regarding the western nations as a whole, the future historian will certainly look upon the first decade of this century as the turning point of modern history. Until then the tide of western expansion was flowing. The British, for example, made their last deliberate colonial acquisitions in 1909. Their impetus had by then been practically lost, the mood for adventure being replaced by an urge to defend, exploit and enjoy. This change of mood found its expression in the Liberal-Labour victory of 1905, which brought into office some who were indifferent and others who were actively hostile to colonial interests. Future emphasis was to be on social welfare not upon imperial expansion. The general situation was one which brought the alternatives into sharp focus. British naval predominance, maintained for a century after the Battle of Trafalgar, was being challenged by Germany. To meet that threat and to maintain the impetus of British expansion in the Far East would have involved providing two separate battle fleets, one based on Britain and the other on the China coast. The one would have to be related to the naval strength of Germany, the other to the naval strength of Japan. Such beyond question was the price of empire.

This price the British electorate refused to pay. Those who had voted the Liberals into office did so under banners promising peace, retrenchment and reform but with ex-

pectation in fact of social benefits to come. To provide both the battleships and the benefits was hardly possible, and it was perfectly clear which policy the people preferred. The Far East Fleet was withdrawn in 1905 and never replaced, a cause of the defeat at Coronel, a cause later on of the loss of the *Prince of Wales* and the *Repulse*. The issue in the Cabinet, doubtful for a time, was settled by the illness and death of the Prime Minister, Sir Henry Campbell-Bannerman, whose successor, Mr. H. H. Asquith, was less restrained in his liberalism. More important still, Asquith's promotion brought the more radical Mr. Lloyd George into office as Chancellor of the Exchequer. From April, 1908, retrenchment was a thing of the past. There was to by social democracy instead and an attack on privilege. The international implications of this policy are hardly relevant to the present theme. More to our purpose is the question of finance and revenue. It is one thing, in principle, to ask from the wealthier citizens a disproportionate contribution toward "common defense and *general* welfare." It is another thing to ask them to contribute directly toward the welfare of those less prosperous. And that was the theme discernible in the hymns which Mr. Lloyd George sang to the accompaniment of his harmonium.

Mr. Lloyd George introduced his first Budget on April 29, 1909. In the course of a speech which lasted four and a half hours, he explained his purpose with fervor. "This is a war budget," he emphasized. "It is for raising money to wage implacable warfare against poverty and squalidness." The main features of the Budget were as follows:

(a) Income tax raised from 1s. to 1s.2d.
(b) Supertax introduced at the rate of 6d. in the pound on incomes over £5000, leviable on the excess over £3000; a tax to which some 10,000 people might be liable.
(c) Heavier death duties. These had already been increased in 1907, with 15 per cent as the maximum. The new maximum was 25 per cent.
(d) A tax on increased land values (destined for considerable amendment in committee).

This Finance Bill was promptly rejected by the House of Lords, as something for which the government had no mandate, and Parliament was accordingly dissolved. In the general election which followed the Liberals were again returned but with a barely adequate majority. The House of Lords nevertheless allowed the Bill to pass and it became law on April 29, 1910. There followed the constitutional crisis of 1911 as a result of which the powers of the House of Lords were drastically curtailed.

An odd feature of the supertax, later to be called the surtax, was that its collection was entrusted to an entirely new branch of the Inland Revenue Department. This branch still exists, so that the work of persecuting the more prosperous taxpayers is actually done twice over by two different sets of people; the cost of collection being roughly doubled. As the collection of rates (local taxes) is entrusted, for no very obvious reason, to yet a third organization, the expense of raising the national and local revenue has never been inconsiderable and shows little tendency to diminish.

Much of the controversy arising from the Budget of 1909 is to be explained with reference to the taxes it imposed. Much also arose, however, from the proposed items of expense. The additional eighteen millions were to be spent as follows:

Old age pensions	£8,750,000
Navy	3,000,000
Minor increases in various departments	1,500,000
Improvement of roads	600,000
To establish labor exchanges	100,000
Development grant	200,000
Land valuation	250,000
Grant to local authorities	300,000

It will be clear from these figures that the increased expenditure on the Navy was relatively small, although soon destined to rise. Old age pensions, by contrast, were ex-

TAXES
Osborn

pensive even in theory and turned out to be still more expensive in practice, reaching £12,415,000 in the first year. At a time when there seemed every likelihood of war with Germany, Mr. Lloyd George had declared war against squalor and incidentally against the wealthier British taxpayers. Of the two, it was the latter war which proved the easier to win.

There may have been many who did not see the significance of the 1909 Budget. There were certainly many who did, more especially when the revenue for 1910-11 proved to be £175,162,000 as compared with the £105,-230,000 of 1909-10. Archer Wilde, for example, pointed out that national and local expenditure totaled £7.10.0. per head of the population, £13.0.0. per working adult, and 16 per cent (rising to 17½ per cent) of the national income. M. Paul Leroy Beaulieu, the French economist, wrote of the Lloyd George Budget, "If this is not Socialism . . . it is the precursor and preparation for it." As accurately, Mr. Edwin A. Pratt wrote that Britain had reached the parting of the ways and that the choice made would be momentous for the future "not alone of the English people, but of the Empire itself." Lord Rosebery pointed out that the yield from death duties was already beginning to diminish, as the estates themselves diminished, and that this confiscated capital was being spent as income.

It would be reasonable to ask at this stage what the reaction was of those whose wealth was thus being threatened. Had capital begun to flee the country? The answer is that the wealthy and even for that matter the very moderately prosperous had long since resorted to income-tax avoidance and evasion, as a result of which the tax incidence was less lethal than it was intended to be. Mr. J. C. L. Zorn came to some interesting conclusions on this subject. For the purposes of his study he divided income-tax payers into two classes, 187,000 with over £1000 a year and ten times that number with less. The former class underpaid its tax, he calculated, by about 27 per cent and the latter by 46 per cent; the very rich, however, avoided 36 per cent of the tax they should have paid. A tax of theoretically 1s. in the pound imposed an average burden of 7¾d. in the pound but the tax fell most heavily on those in the middle of the range, the salaried people whose income was more or less known. Death duties could also be avoided by deeds of gift, a device which was less widely used than might have been expected; the result, no doubt, of so many people having been made to read *King Lear* at an impressionable age. That the tax was so much less than it appeared to be was in part the cause of its being sustained with relative calm and collected with comparative ease. Some of the ablest people were paying least and some of the richest not paying at all.

In the same year that the principle of disproportional income tax was being introduced into Britain, income tax was being introduced afresh in the United States under President Taft. In the light of the Supreme Court's ruling of 1894, this could be done only by amending the Constitution. Such an amendment was duly prepared, and the whole campaign stage-managed, by Representative Cordell Hull from Tennessee. It was he who briefed Senator Bailey of Texas and it was he who made a preliminary study of the tax systems already in existence. Congress voted 318 to 14 for the Sixteenth Amendment. It had then to be approved by the states, a process which took some years, six states failing to take action or refusing to ratify. The Amendment became law on February 25, 1913, and was put into effect in the revenue bill of that year. Cordell

Hull, who has been called the "mastermind" in this affair and who was certainly the acknowledged expert on taxation, had all along favored a flat rate. At this point, however, Representative John Nance Garner of Texas succeeded in gaining acceptance for the principle of graduation. Lenin prophesied that the United States would spend itself to destruction. Toward that end this graduated tax was the first and essential step.

The American income tax of 1913 contained all the principles of taxation by then accepted in Britain, but the immediate incidence was relatively light. A tax of 1 per cent was levied on the net taxable income of every citizen or resident, with a personal exemption of $3000. The system of graduation was represented by a surtax payable on incomes of $20,000 and over. Beginning at a mere 1 per cent, this was to reach 6 per cent on incomes of $500,000 and upward; not a very onerous tax in itself but a foretaste of all that was to follow. So it came about that the United States entered World War I, as did Britain, with the machinery for expanding its revenue to meet the crisis. What it lacked, and what all countries lacked, was a machinery for contracting its revenue after the crisis was past.

Compared with the United States the position of Great Britain in 1909 was far less favorable, if only because it was further down the same road. Its budget was already incompatible with scientific finance. As Mr. W. R. Lawson observed, "In its inception, its spirit, its objects, and its methods it is sentimental rather than financial." This was profoundly true, with the result that Britain was the most heavily taxed of the world powers and yet militarily weak in proportion to its expenditure. In total national taxation the British figure of £3.6.3. per head was to be compared with £2.16.1. in France, £1.4.7. in the United States, 18s.4d. in Germany and 12s.4d. in Japan. The British revenue from taxation came to £151,955,000 ($425,474,000) whereas the revenue of the United States, with nearly double the population, came to only £109,384,916 ($306,277,764). The effect of piling war taxes upon this peacetime level of exaction was to mean the eventual ruin of the class upon which Britain relied for leadership. It was to mean the collapse of the British Empire; a collapse which many of Mr. Lloyd George's supporters would rather welcome than otherwise. It was to mean a great deal more than was immediately foreseen.

There is nothing in these figures to prevent the reader from believing, as many people did and do, that measures of social welfare are more valuable than battleships. Given a straight choice, many would still decide in favor of old age pensions. In practice, of course, the choice was never as clear as we can now make it seem, and the result was the sort of compromise we have learned to expect. Few realized all the implications of what they were doing. Nor, had they done so, was everyone's object the same. To one it was all-important that Britain should show the world an example of social progress. To others it was self-evident that a lack of warships would eventually leave Britain without the means to pay for the welfare measures which were theoretically desirable. The final irony of the situation was that a drastic curtailment of administrative costs might have allowed Britain to afford both labor exchanges and guns. That, however, was a secret known to very few. For the public at large the choice was broadly between cruisers and schools and it was upon this choice that the Empire's future would depend.

The fate of the British Empire was decided, in effect, by the relative levels of expenditure shown in the following table:

Year	The Navy	Social Welfare[1]
1904-5	£41,062,075	£15,160,642
1905-6	37,159,235	15,934,282
1906-7	34,599,541	16,477,141
1907-8	32,735,767	16,892,714
1908-9	33,511,719	18,925,318
1909-10	36,059,652	25,924,148
1910-11	41,118,668	28,031,508
1911-12	44,882,047	30,381,777
1912-13	45,616,540	35,582,128

[1] Including Old Age Pensions, Education and Labor Exchanges.

Here the second column represents the margin of British superiority at the Battle of Jutland and the absence of the force which would have turned defeat into victory at Coronel. The third column explains where the money had gone and how the total came to be as large as it was.

There is, however, another aspect of the matter to which little attention has been paid. To maintain a string of tropical dependencies, scattered along the vital trade routes, the primary need was admittedly for the warships which were missing after 1905, but the secondary need was for the men who would give their working lives to the dependencies themselves. The need was then for soldiers, administrators, engineers, physicians and planters. These had been forthcoming in quantity since 1600 but it was essential to the system that those who survived should come back to Britain on retirement. In no other way could the next generation be endowed with the same energy and continuity of outlook. So the British exile was a man who looked forward all his life to a certain kind of reward. Fiercely devoted as he might be, and usually was, to the land in which his active career was spent, his final goal was a home in Britain. As those who survived to reach home were about 10 per cent of those who went abroad the earlier adventurers expected a proportionate reward. The penniless younger brother might end as landowner, churchwarden and justice of the peace. As generations passed, the risks diminished and the expectations of the returning exile were proportionately less. But the minimum expectation to the end was a villa at Torquay and the majority dreamed rather of a country place with some rough shooting and a stream in which to fish. The incidence of taxation in the present century combined with other social changes to make this dream unattainable. To maintain a county family was difficult, to found one almost impossible. The returned builder of empire was more likely to end in a London suburb, talking to his bored neighbors about the past glories of Colombo or Rangoon. This was no advertisement for the Empire and it would decide his friends against letting their boys go, as they had planned, to Trinidad or Fiji.

The Welfare State reacted on the Empire in another way, for the money taken from the returned exile was to make Britain more comfortable for those who might otherwise have gone abroad. While there were diminished prospects for those who went, there were diminished hardships for those who stayed behind. To gain independent means and to pay for the children's education was no longer necessary and might not even be possible. As a breed, the builders of empire have become extinct. Success in the modern age is to be measured by one's ability to give the minimum of effort to one's career and extract the maximum of subsidy from the state. To these ends a new generation was to devote itself, leaving the British Empire to collapse more suddenly and more completely than any undefeated empire of the past; an example to the world of what excessive taxation can bring about and in how short a time. For this and for a variety of other reasons, the year 1909 should be firmly underlined in the historical textbooks of the future.

It is the fashion to ascribe this collapse to the forces of nationalism and democracy. It can be argued that Britain has withdrawn gracefully from territories which have become ripe for democratic self-government, owing their political education to British instruction and example. In this version of events there would seem to be an element of truth and any amount of convenience, but the true proportions only time will show. The value of democracy to those whose manifest destiny is to fall under the rule of another and less benevolent empire is not always apparent. Its value to those who confer such a doubtful blessing is less open to dispute. The money saved can be spent on social surveys and social reforms at home. It is in this sense that the farewell empire is the logical sequel to the welfare state. What looks to some like generosity may look to others like betrayal.

This trend in Britain has its American equivalent. The same sort of retreat from heroic action to the cramped comforts of a timid security can be seen also in the United States. The period of adventure lies in the past when it was not so much a continent to be won as a fortune to be made that drove the railroads from coast to coast. Now the railroads are being taxed into a surly obsolescence that will lead inevitably to nationalization; and the highways network that must take their place is being built, of necessity, at the taxpayer's cost. Private enterprise is dwindling and public effort can seldom be described as enterprise. Bountiful as American industry may be, its characteristic achievements lie today in the endless provision of automatic washing machines and backyard swimming pools. Good as they may be, these products afford no proof in themselves of national greatness or vigor. There is in them no epic quality to fire the imagination or teach a future age that we of today were men indeed.

There used to be a nursery legend about the antidote being found near the poison, a theory deriving little support from either experience or science. It was pointed out, for example, that dock leaves were usually to be found near a bed of stinging nettles, and that dock leaves were the very thing to apply when stung. There were further theories, no doubt, to explain why the Providence which thought of the dock leaf should not have saved trouble in the first instance by doing without the nettle. It all probably pointed to some valuable moral, if only we could remember what. Evidence to support this general theory would seem in general to be conspicuously lacking but there sometimes appears a crumb of information which might be used in an argument on the subject.

The history of taxation is a case in point. It was in the year 1909 that the English-speaking world took certain major fiscal decisions which, logically pursued, could lead only to financial ruin. By one of those startling coincidences which science would forbid us to describe as providential, it was in 1909 that the present author was born.

5

RECENT HISTORY

To pay for World War I the British income tax was raised to 5s. on earned incomes over £2500 or unearned incomes over £2000, but by 1918 the standard rate stood at 6s. with supertax payable on incomes over £2500. Other countries began collecting income tax at about this period, France in 1914, Australia in 1916, Canada in 1917. It was the tendency of the age. Other countries had begun the practice earlier and taxes on the disproportionate principle were soon being collected in Switzerland, the Netherlands, New Zealand and elsewhere. There were optimists who imagined that taxes would be reduced as soon as war ended. But this did not happen. On the one hand, war expenditure continued after the armistice; on the other, peacetime government expenditure rose to meet the wartime revenue. And whereas the yield of British income tax and supertax in 1913-14 had been £47,249,000, the estimate for 1920-21 provided for no less than £387,000,000 — the Budget itself reaching a total of £1,532,324,000. There was a general and rather curious expectation that the world was to be improved by the outcome of the war and that any and every welfare scheme was financially possible. The standard rate of income tax was reduced to 4s.6d. by 1926 but rose again to 5s. in 1931-34, and to 5s.6d. in 1938. The beginning of World War II was to find Britain paying taxes at almost the rate as levied at the conclusion of World War I.

Interestingly, the belligerent country which recovered most rapidly after World War I was Belgium. Occupation by the Germans had saved the Belgians from the vast expansion of government activities which afflicted the powers understood to have been victorious. The Belgians had no network of regulations, no horde of officials — no tottering and expensive superstructure from which to free themselves. Nor had they convinced each other that peace would bring the millennium with it. Unhampered by a wartime bureaucracy, they set to work and regained their former prosperity with surprising ease. The same could not be said of Britain, where the government share of the national income, nearly 15 per cent in 1913, rose to over 28 per cent in 1932 and to over 30 per cent in 1938, by which year the scale of private new investment (except in houses) had dwindled to nearly nothing. Nor was the situation in the United States so markedly different. Whereas the federal government spent about one billion dollars in 1914, its expenditure after World War I, in 1924, was just over four times as much. Surtax had been introduced in 1918, being graduated from 1 per cent to 65 per cent, so that net incomes of more than one million dollars were taxed at 77 per cent, the highest rate then known. Tax rates were lowered in 1926-28 but raised again in 1932-37, by which latter year surtaxes reached a record maximum of 75 per cent. Internal revenue which stood a little over one and a half billion in 1932 came to over thirteen billion by 1942.

One of the oddest features of American taxation was the creation of the Intelligence Unit of the United States Treasury Department. This organization was founded in 1919 for the general purpose of preventing tax evasion. The theory was, no doubt, that agents of this unit would confront Vanderbilts and Guggenheims before a grand jury, proving beyond possibility of doubt that their tax returns were false. They may have done this repeatedly but it is not for this that they will be remembered in either prose or verse. For it was they, and they alone, who tamed the gangsters between 1930 and about 1936. It is ironical that it should have been so. The murders attributed to the

Al Capone gang of Chicago numbered 46 in 1925 and 64 in the following year. There were gang battles fought in the streets with armored cars on either side. A reign of terror lasted until the year 1931, when Al Capone was brought to trial, fined $50,000 (which he could well afford) and sentenced to eleven years imprisonment. He was not convicted of murder, robbery, riot and graft. His conviction was for failure to pay his income tax, having filed no return and paid no tax in respect of the years 1924-29, a period during which his income was said to have varied between $100,000 and $257,000 a year. It was proved, beyond question, that his taxes were in arrears to the amount of $215,030 and 48 cents.

This case is cited as typical rather than exceptional, for the same fate befell Waxey Gordon, the New York gangster. Tom Pendergast, moreover, political boss of Kansas City, was proved to have spent $693,234 in 1935; a year during which his declared income was $125,633. Enoch Johnson, the dictator of Atlantic City, was finally jailed for ten years, again as a result of investigation by the tax expert. It is true that Huey Long died before he could be prosecuted for tax evasion but his associate, Dr. James Monroe Smith, President of Louisiana State University, was less fortunate. Smith was proved to have had a share in the vast profit made by the university's architects, and all this without confiding in the tax authorities. Many other criminals shared Dr. Smith's fate without sharing his academic rank, and there has been very general agreement that they were undesirable characters who fully deserved the penalties they incurred. The doubt remains, however, as to whether or not they were indicted for the wrong offense.

Granted, however, that there were anomalies in the methods of tax enforcement used, it can hardly be said that the population of the United States was heavily taxed on the eve of World War II. Income tax was paid by some four or five million taxpayers and yielded only about 20 per cent of the national revenue. None was paid in 1932-39 by those with an income of under $2500. Thereafter the level at which incomes were exempt was steadily lowered, to $2000 in 1940, to $1500 in 1941, to $1200 in 1942, and to $642 in 1943. Unfortunately for the taxpayers in both Britain and U.S.A., these exactions were cleverly concealed. As the tax gatherer reached levels of the population that were scarcely literate he adopted the device of making the employer do the tax collection at his own expense, and to many working men and women, tax deductions in this form were not very perceptible.

By about 1950 the privilege of paying United States income tax had been extended to some fifty million people, increasing tenfold the number of those who had formerly to pay. United States taxes reached an unprecedented level in 1951 when it was discovered by Miss Vivien Kellems that President Harry S. Truman had, in a little over six years, taxed the country $12 billion more than all the previous Presidents combined, from George Washington down to Franklin D. Roosevelt. Truman demanded $260 billion whereas his predecessors had taken only $248 billion among them. Although by 1955 the figure for exemption had risen to $2000 a year, all incomes above that level were paying 20 per cent, the percentage rising steeply until incomes of $16,000 were paying 50 per cent and incomes of $50,000 no less than 75 per cent, with 87 per cent as the maximum at the highest levels. It is also significant that

President Eisenhower, who twice campaigned strongly for government economy and lower taxes, has actually exceeded Truman's record and with no war as an excuse. This is yet another illustration of the inexorability of Parkinson's Second Law which operates in spite of party philosophy or personal preference.

But the taxes which in the United States were onerous, in Britain were lethal. With a high rate of taxation even when World War II began, with a longer period of war and with cities heavily damaged by bombing, the British would have been financially crippled in any case. Matters had been made infinitely worse, however, by the incidence of Socialism and imperial defense, the dual burden assumed in 1909. On the one hand the Conservatives were trying to save what remained of the Empire; on the other, the Labour Party was building a Socialist Utopia. No country in the world could have afforded both, and some doubted whether Britain could afford either. During the war the standard rate of income tax rose quickly, first to 7s. in the pound in 1939, to 7s.6d. and later to 8s.6d. in 1940, finally to 10s. (or 50 per cent) in 1942. Surtax was imposed on incomes over £2000, scaled from 5s.9d. to 8s.3d. (at £5000) and so to 9s.6d. on incomes of £10,000 and over. The result was that beyond a certain level incomes were being taxed at 19s.6d. in the pound, a rate stopping just short of total confiscation. Death duties were scaled up to reach over 40 per cent on estates of £300,000 and over 65 per cent on the largest estates of all. Nor was this colossal burden much reduced when the war came to an end. The twofold expenditure continued and was in some ways increased.

Efforts to save the Empire included warfare in Malaya, Korea, Cyprus and Egypt, with garrisons, subsidies and cultural representatives elsewhere. The new utopia in Britain involved a civil service which had mysteriously increased in numbers from 387,000 in 1939 to 704,000 in 1945, and a series of nationalized industries run for the most part at a substantial loss. What this meant in taxation and death duties might be imagined even if it were not known. To take for example a married couple with two children and no unearned income, these would in 1950-51 pay income and surtax on the following scale:

Income	Tax
£1,000	£168.15.0.
£2,000	£528.15.0.
£4,000	£1716. 5.0.
£5,000	£2391. 5.0.
£10,000	£6316. 5.0.
£20,000	£15591. 5.0.
£50,000	£44841. 5.0.
£100,000	£93591. 5.0.

Thus not even the wealthiest could, by legal means, have more than £5000 to £6400 of spendable income.

The tax situation would have been bad enough had income and surtax been all, but to these had been added a variety of other taxes, direct and indirect. There was the purchase tax, the national health and insurance contributions and the greatly increased local rates. Tax had been piled on tax; and one result of death duties (amounting to £2000 million between 1945 and 1957) was so to lessen the number of the rich that the tax burden had increasingly to fall on the poor. Wrote Vivien Kellems on this subject in *Toil, Taxes and Trouble* (1952):

> Take a look at England. The incomes of the rich and upper classes have shrivelled under the blighting hand of the tax collector until they are practically non-existent, and the heavy tax burden is rapidly shifting to the shoulders of the working people who are supposed to reap only benefits from English Socialism. In eleven short years, from 1938 to 1949, total taxes from incomes below £1000 leaped 615 per cent, while those from incomes over that amount increased 171.

This tax situation created anomalies at either end of the scale. Viscount Chandos could complain that his actual emoluments as a Director of Imperial Chemicals were a little over one-third of the new office boy's net weekly pay. On the other hand the workman could complain that the £2 he was paid for overtime on Saturday was 26s. by the time he received it. Supposing, moreover, that he spent that 26s. on cigarettes and a half bottle of gin, another 20s. would go to Customs and Excise, bringing his real earnings down to 6s. In dollars and cents this would be the equivalent of having some $1.50 left over from a $10 bill. The inflationary effect of such taxation is obvious. There have been some tax concessions of late, with the standard rate of income tax reduced from 8s.6d. to 7s.9d. in 1959. But the significant observation made on that year's budget came from Mr. Gaitskell, Leader of the Opposition, who is reported as saying that "the Budget involved giving away not far short of £400 million. Any Chancellor who could give this away could be described as lucky."

The words "give away" reveal, unconsciously, an attitude of mind. By communist teaching, the whole wealth of the country belongs to the government, which *gives away* a proportion of it to the more deserving of its subjects. The whole idea of private property is a thing of the past, the state owns all. Fortunate is the Chancellor who can be fairly generous; such generosity may not be possible another year. On this subject Edmund Burke thought differently.

> To provide for us in our necessities is not in the power of Government. It would be a vain presumption in statesmen to think they can do it. The people maintain them, and not they the people. It is in the power of Government to prevent much evil; it can do very little positive good in this or perhaps in anything else.

Much might be said on this subject of the government's universal ownership but there is another aspect of the 1959-60 Budget which might seem of more immediate importance. Here was the Leader of the Opposition chiding the Chancellor of the Exchequer for his reckless generosity toward the taxpayer, the Chancellor himself maintaining that his generosity was justified in the circumstances of the day. But what generosity (let alone what recklessness) was there to discuss? The total revenue was expected to reach £5,620,000,000 and the government proposed to spend £5,223,000,000 of it. This is to be compared with the British revenue of £181,710,000 in the far more prosperous days of 1909-10. It is to be compared again with the government expenditure of £1,532,324,000 in 1920-21, or even with the revenue of £1,021,000,000 in 1938 and £4,022,-000,000, of 1948. With the exception of the budgets for 1955-58, the budget under discussion is the heaviest ever laid in peacetime on the long-suffering public. It comes to more than the gross national product of 1938. And while the central and local governments took nearly a third of the

Taxation

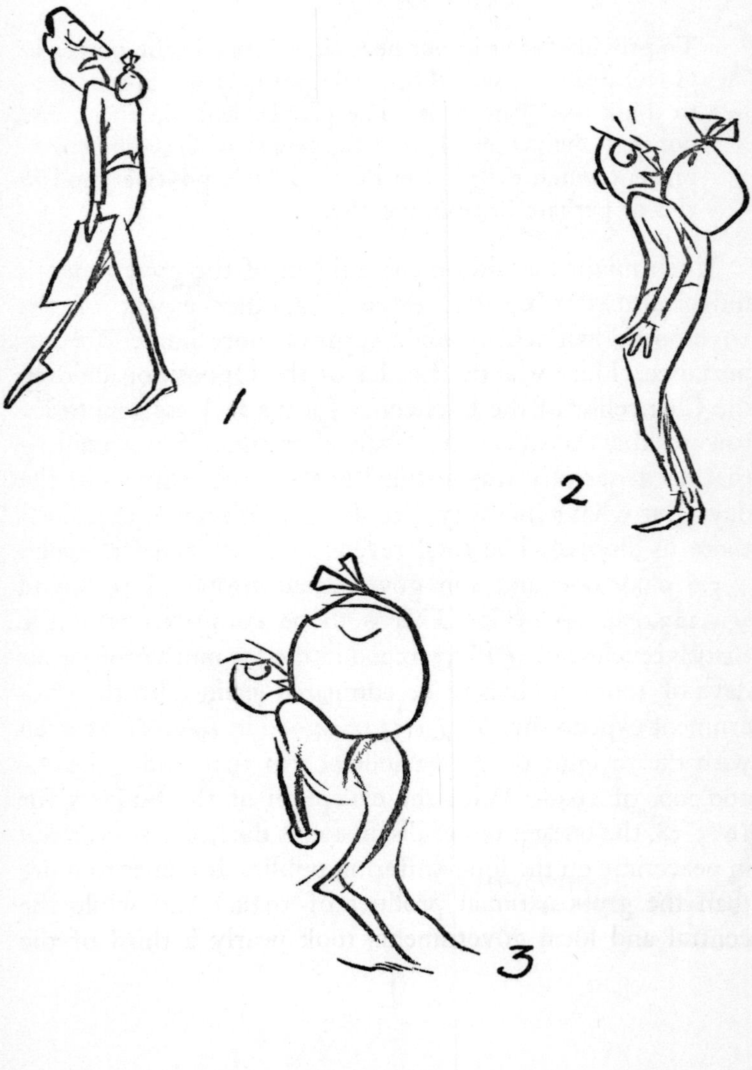

4

5

6

gross national product in 1957, there is no reason to think that their share will be notably smaller in 1959. The statistics of British central and local government expenditure have become a sort of nightmare.

The American who reads this commentary on British finance may feel that his own country is further from disaster; and it is, strictly speaking, true. But his sense of satisfaction will dwindle when he comes to study the figures. With the federal government taking from 20 to 87 per cent of the taxpayer's income, and with state and local taxes to be added to the burden, it is obvious that the United States has taken the same road but has not progressed down it quite so far. In theory it should be possible to reverse or stop, but there are economists at hand who ask rather for acceleration. They contrast the American expenditure on privately produced and marketed goods with the American niggardliness in providing for the public service. They call for higher taxation as a means of redressing the balance. They regard the sales tax as a particularly hopeful method of making private goods more expensive and public services more abundant. There is much that is plausible in the arguments used and especially plausible to those unacquainted with postwar Britain. But these experts take no account of the tendency of taxes to increase by the law that governs their expansion, nor do they attempt to fix the point at which further taxation becomes disastrous.

Were some limit established at which taxation must stop, were a barrier built across the road at some point this side of the precipice, the arguments for expanding the public services would be more plausible still. Their fallacy lies in the assumption that a higher expenditure produces a better result. But this does not follow. Artists and craftsmen know that there is a virtue in the resistance of their material. A statue made of granite has a quality not discoverable in a statue made of butter. The resistance of the architect's material is represented (in part) by the factor of cost. The intrusion of this factor produces a better building than could have been produced in its absence. Where there is no ceiling to the cost, the architect merely goes off his head. What is true of architecture is true also of administration. The economical solution is also the best, call-

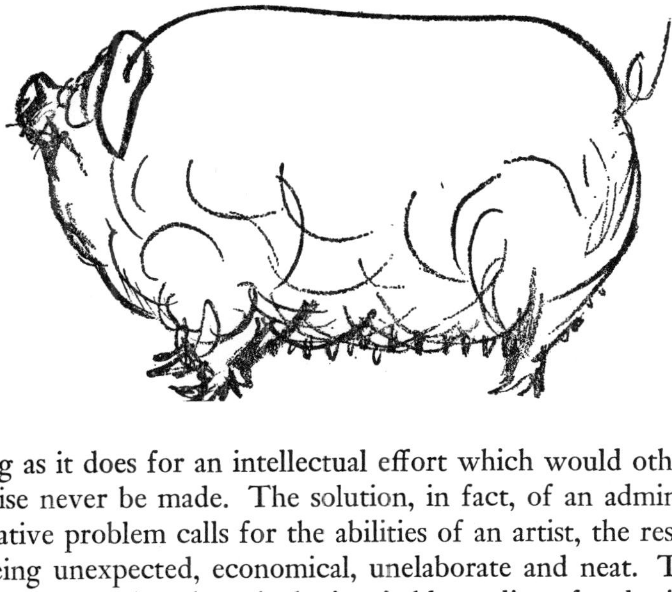

ing as it does for an intellectual effort which would otherwise never be made. The solution, in fact, of an administrative problem calls for the abilities of an artist, the result being unexpected, economical, unelaborate and neat. The final answer has about it the inevitable quality of a classical composition, a quality to which the resistance of the material is vital.

There are those who argue that we have reached a level of affluence at which administrative extravagance is within

our means, or is necessary, even, to ensure employment for all. Arguments such as these ignore both the fact and the nature of waste. A Goldbergian solution to a real problem would be artistically unforgivable even were it financially sound. Such arguments also ignore the loss of efficiency which arises from a bureaucracy's growth. Where there is no automatic check on this growth, the raising of further taxes and the allocation of larger sums will bring us nothing but increased frustration. Even were it probable, however, that increased expenditure would buy anything but administrative constipation, the fact remains that the precipice lies somewhere ahead. We know of its existence from the fate of earlier travelers on this road. We even know roughly where it is. All that remains to do is to build our barrier at the proper place.

6

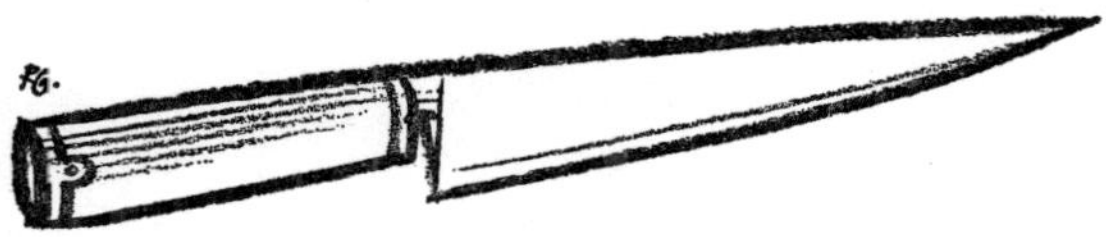

THE LIMITS OF TAXATION

TAXES can be grouped, as we have seen, into two broad categories, those we impose on ourselves and those we inflict upon other people. Taxes in the first category, examples of which in history are extremely rare, are self-limiting. They may rise in a time of emergency but, once the crisis is past, they should tend to fall. The United States in their earlier days offered an example of taxation falling within this category. Nineteenth-century Britain offered another such example, at least for a time, and other instances are known in both the ancient and modern periods of history. On the other hand, most taxes clearly come within the category of burdens imposed by some people upon others. The taxes decreed by ancient monarchies were all of this type and so are the graduated taxes of today at all levels above the average; being voted, indirectly at least, by those to whom the heaviest rates will not apply.

The taxes inflicted by some people upon others will inevitably rise as expenditure rises, and expenditure will rise in accordance with Parkinson's Second Law. Their only limit is at the point where the victim refuses to pay, and to that point they will rise by the principle which governs their growth. In ancient times that point of refusal was reached when the tax demand rose much above 10 per cent of the gross product. Our information is admittedly meager, but such figures as we possess range between 5 and 10 per cent except in cases where the entire economy is known to have collapsed. Now it is obvious that the amount of the tax will be something a little above the cost of its avoidance. For a customs duty 2½ per cent was originally the natural limit, and about 10 per cent for a tax on land. That level must have been related to the cost and the risk of migrating elsewhere. An early example of such a migration is to be found in the Book of Exodus. Pharaoh taxed the Israelites in terms of service. "And the Egyptians made the children of Israel to serve with rigor: and they made their lives bitter with hard bondage, in mortar, and in brick, and in all manner of service in the field." At some point unspecified in this raising of the assessment, the Israelites judged that the time had come to go elsewhere. In nineteenth-century Malaya the Chinese tin miners would yield a Malay chief up to 10 per cent of their output as payment for "protection." If he asked more they drifted to another minefield, where the chief asked less. Some chiefs reacted to this very much as Pharaoh did and with about as much result. As a reckless generalization we can say that the productive people of the world have discovered from experience that they will always have to yield 10 per cent to somebody, whether to a gangster, a feudal lord or a department of internal revenue. It comes to much the same thing in any case. To escape from one tax gatherer will usually mean paying blackmail to another. Up to about 10 per cent the exaction is in accordance, it would seem, with a law of nature. When it rises much above that level, the time has come for the Israelites to study the atlas. There may be better places than Egypt; and in point of fact there are.

In studying the history of public finance the temptation is to conclude that people are willing to pay taxes up to a certain point; up to 10 per cent for example. This would be an entirely mistaken idea. Normal people are reluctant to pay any tax of any proportion at any time. Their grievance will be just as vocal whether the taxes are heavy or light. The Chinese never regarded payment of a tenth as "perfectly just and equitable" whatever any scholar may say to the contrary. But they did regard such a tax as inevitable and customary. Now, in noting the resignation of ancient taxpayers, we should also note the circumstances which limited their liability. For, under the empires of Rome and China, migration at least between provinces was relatively easy. The situation is entirely different when there is nowhere to go, when taxation elsewhere is just as bad. In these radically altered circumstances the barrier at 10 per cent is removed and taxes will rise to a new maximum. Within the rigid frontiers of modern nationalism, for example, the taxpayer is indeed captive. His taxes will rise, therefore, until they reach a new point of refusal. At what level is this point to be found?

This important question was discussed by that able Victorian economist, J. R. McCulloch, who wrote as follows:

> Oppression, it has been said, either raises men into heroes or sinks them into slaves; and taxation, according to its magnitude and the mode in which it is imposed, either makes men industrious, enterprising and wealthy, or indolent, dispirited and impoverished.

McCulloch here judges the limit of taxable capacity by the reaction of the taxpayers, which might obviously vary with other circumstances. It is clear, however, from his subsequent remarks, that he was contemplating taxes within a certain range. He thus expected to find great resistance to a direct tax amounting to between 10 and 15 per cent of the taxpayer's income — such resistance indeed as to make it a tax on honesty and a bounty on fraud.

> . . . were it carried to any great height, or to 10, 15 or 20 per cent, it could generate the most barefaced prostitution of principle, and do much to sap that nice sense of honour which is the only sure foundation of national probity and virtue.

McCulloch's conclusion on this subject was more than borne out by experience. The reaction of the taxpayer who cannot escape the tax by migration is to reduce it by some other form of avoidance. We have seen (p. 59) that British taxpayers of 1909 were thought thus to have reduced their theoretical tax of 1s. to 7¾d. in the pound. Above 10 per cent the effort to avoid the tax is intensified, as the time and trouble spent yields a better return than would the effort to have made additional income, itself again subject to the tax. It is clear that a direct tax of from 10 to 20 per cent of the taxpayer's income tends to deflect initiative and ingenuity into a new channel and one quite profitless to the community as a whole. More than that, the brains devoted to tax avoidance have to be matched by the brains devoted to tax collection. And despite all the official ingenuity displayed, each tax increase yields a poorer result than the last. The point might be reached, at least in theory, when no further tax increase would improve the revenue. Before that point is reached, however, the situation would have been transformed in another way.

What happens when direct taxation takes as much as 25 per cent of the national income was first noticed by Lord Keynes in about 1923. It was he who pointed out that taxation beyond a certain point is the cause of inflation. When there is a high tax on the profits of industry, employers can reduce the tax by distributing the profits among their staff; a form of generosity which costs little. With this lessened resistance to wage demands, the value of the currency declines. One way in which profits can be distributed is through entertainment. Some American observers have already called attention to the inflationary effect of the "expense account economy." Many minor executives prefer a generous expense account to a raise in salary which would be heavily taxed and more soberly spent. It is they who support the so-called "expense account restaurants," places of exotic décor where patrons lunch in a darkness which is all but complete. They cannot see to read the prices on the menu but these, in the special circumstances, are irrelevant. For the company, it is a less expensive form of remuneration. For the community it is yet another, if minor, cause of inflation. As inflation progresses, a policy of devaluation then finds general support, with the result that the state's creditors, the investors in government stock, are cheated in what has become the normal fashion. Writing off a proportion of the national debt, the state becomes solvent again and the real value of the taxes will begin to fall.

The argument, as put forward by Colin Clark in 1945, is that taxation exceeding 25 per cent of the national income must defeat its own purpose. This argument attracted considerable notice at the time but was not generally agreed among economists. While many experts admitted that some sort of limit must exist, they considered that this could vary according to national character and other circumstances. The late Sir Stafford Cripps is known to have believed that the British would bear almost limitless taxation, and this is clearly the assumption that underlies British financial policy. And those who share Cripps's belief can point to the British record since 1939. The tax collectors of Britain (central and local) who took 25.4 per cent of the national income in 1938 and 39.8 per cent in 1947, were actually taking a larger share (40.1 per cent) in 1950 and no economic catastrophe had ensued. The whole subject was discussed at the 1953 Symposium of the Tax Institute, most delegates to which more or less agreed that Britain is taxing itself to death. Few, however, were prepared to say at what point rising taxation should have been checked, and fewer still would have agreed on a rule applicable to all countries at all periods of history.

One thing apparent from all discussions on this subject is that people will pay heavy taxes when fighting for their existence. When the alternative appears to be national destruction, taxes of up to 50 per cent of the national income may well be paid without much complaint. The point of refusal is reached only when the doubt arises as to whether existence is worth while. It is also apparent that the atmosphere of crisis can be retained to some extent after the war is over. Appeals to patriotism can still be made, with promises of a better world to come. There is no particular reason for supposing that an orgy of mutual destruction should result in a better world, but the promise is often made and often believed. In Britain at least, taxes amounting to 40 per cent of the national income have been paid without protest for a number of years. The temptation among those responsible is to assume that all is well and that comparable taxes can be borne indefinitely. In fact, however, the results of oppressive taxation are cumulative and slow. Historical examples serve to illustrate a strangling process spread over many years. Today the tempo is quickened but not so much as to be readily perceptible. It is the more important, therefore, to note the symptoms which mark the progress of the disease. They represent the loss, successively, of influence, freedom and stability.

Loss of influence follows from loss of strength. Among some of the potential belligerents of 1909 the figures for total taxation were as follows:

	Population (to nearest 1000)	Taxation in £ sterling	In U. S. Dollars at 4.75 to £.
United Kingdom	45,469,000	£151,955,000	$721,786,250
France	39,252,000	£111,686,082	$530,508,885
Austria-Hungary	51,251,000	£ 95,055,544	$451,513,796
United States	88,926,000	£109,384,916	$519,578,351
Germany	63,879,000	£ 88,055,333	$418,262,832
Russia	160,095,000	£ 72,853,500	$346,063,625
Italy	34,270,000	£ 50,577,962	$240,245,320
Japan	53,273,000	£ 32,831,510	$155,949,672

Between these countries there were significant differences in development and wealth. The fact remains, however, that Britain was the country most heavily taxed in the years before World War I, with France a bad second and Austria-Hungary a good third. These were the countries whose influence declined sharply in the years which followed the war. The two countries where taxation was lowest were those whose influence increased the most. By 1938 the most heavily taxed countries were, in the following order, Germany, Britain and France: again the countries whose influence was afterwards to decline. While other factors must have their importance, a country like the United States, which in 1938 combined wealth with a low rate of taxation, was obviously more formidable than a country which was heavily taxed before the war even began. The contrast between high taxable capacity and low taxes is a sign of latent strength and one not wasted on the world at large. Nor will rival powers fail to notice the high level of taxation maintained today in countries like Britain and France. Neither country, they conclude,

I won't permit it!

will ever fight again except in defending its frontiers. A country so placed, with no visible margin of strength, can have only a dwindling influence in international affairs. That such a toothless country will do anything to extend or even secure its wider interests is believed by nobody. It can do little even to maintain the peace. For most purposes it can be simply ignored.

The first effect, then, of a high rate of peacetime taxation is to reduce a country's influence in world affairs. The second effect is to be measured in the loss of individual freedom. On this subject the words of Thomas Jefferson cannot be quoted too often:

> I place economy among the first and most important virtues, and public debt as the greatest of dangers to be feared . . . To preserve our independence, we must not let our rulers load us with public debt . . . We must make our choice between economy and liberty or profusion and servitude.
>
> . . . If we run into such debts, we must be taxed in our meat and drink, in our necessities and comforts, in our labor and in our amusements . . . If we can prevent the Government from wasting the labor of the people, under the pretense of caring for them, they will be happy.

These are prophetic words. Wasting the labors of the people "under the pretense of caring for them" is exactly what our goverments do. Freedom is founded upon ownership of property. It involves self-expression in terms of architecture and art. It cannot exist where the rulers own everything, nor even when they concede some limited right of tenure. But the modern belief (see p. 76) is that spendable income is a concession by the state. The taxation which is intended to promote equality, the taxation which exceeds the real public need, and above all the tax which is so graduated as to prevent the accumulation of private capital, is inconsistent with freedom. Against a state which owns everything, the individual has neither the means of defense nor anything to defend. For the normal human being who is not a creative artist or scientist by profession the means of self-expression consist largely of rooms to modify and gardens to tend, trees to plant and offspring to rear. Losing these opportunities for expression, the individual loses individuality, freedom and hope.

The third effect of a high rate of peacetime taxation is the loss of stability. There are many human achievements, including some of the finest, which need more than a single lifetime for completion. The individual can compose a symphony or paint a canvas, build up a business or restore order in a city. He cannot build a cathedral or grow an avenue of oak trees. Still less can he gain the stature essential to statesmanship in a highly developed and complex society. There is a need for continuity of effort, spread over several generations, and for just such a continuity as governments must lack. Given the party system, more especially, under the democratic form of rule, policy is continually modified or reversed. A family can be biologically stable in a way that a modern legislature is not. It is to families, therefore, that we look for such stability as society may need. But how can the family function if subject to crippling taxes during every lifetime and partial confiscation with every death? How can one generation provide the springboard for the next? Without such a springboard, all must start alike, and none can excel; and where none can excel nothing excellent will result. Without sustained effort, without stability, no civilization can for long survive.

From this analysis it may not seem easy to fix on a certain level of taxation as representing the maximum. So far it would seem that there are successive points at which evil results successively appear. With peacetime taxation amounting to over 10 per cent of the national income, capital will begin to migrate. If its flight is prevented, whether by circumstances or by legislation, taxes can rise to 20 per cent but against a stiffening opposition which takes the form of tax avoidance and evasion carried to the utmost lengths of determination and skill. Above 20 per cent each tax increase will produce proportionately less. Above 25 per cent there is serious inflation, reducing the value of the revenue collected. Above 30 per cent the decline in national influence, observable long before to the expert, becomes obvious to the world at large. At 35 per cent there is a visible decline in freedom and stability. At 36 per cent there is disaster, complete and final although not always immediate. Taxation beyond that point, feasible and perhaps necessary in time of war, is lethal in time of peace. Of the taxation precipice, 36 per cent (for most countries) represents the brink.

In one respect the simile of the precipice is misleading, for the fall of a nation is less dramatic than the fall of a single vehicle or man. It can live for a time on borrowings and capital. There will be a dwindling but still valuable

stock of integrity, enterprise, energy and hope. Older people will go on working from habit even after the younger folk have seen that it is pointless. People will go on saving from habit even after they have seen past savings

shrivel to nothing. People will retain a professional pride for years after they have ceased to retain more than a fraction of their professional fee. The machine goes on for a while even after the power has been switched off. For a time the slowing down is not even perceptible. Then the whine of the engine becomes a throb, the throb becomes a slow pulsation and that becomes in turn a measured and lessening groan and hiss. The blurred flywheel becomes visible, its spokes marking a slower rhythm, and so the engine wheezes and grunts its way to a final grinding, clanging halt. It is the end of the journey and, in this instance, the end of the train.

From this necessarily simplified account of what may be expected to happen there emerges as yet no single, clear rule as to what the ideal rate of taxation ought to be. Nor is the situation made simpler by the fact that some services — education, health and life insurance — would have to be provided by the individual if they were not provided by the state. The extent of these services makes it difficult, even, to compare the weight of taxation as between one country and another. What is clear, however, is that the progressive transference of responsibility from the individual to the state cannot but weaken individuality itself. There is clearly, somewhere, a line to be drawn. The traditional 10 per cent has the support of experience but there may be special reasons for exceeding it. Where these reasons exist, taxation should stop at the point where it absorbs 20 per cent of the national income provided that it is strictly proportionate and that no income suffers direct taxation beyond the limit of 25 per cent. Countries which have recently exceeded the bounds of safety are (in order of extravagance) the United Kingdom, France, New Zealand, Japan and the United States. Some of these may yet struggle back to a position of financial stability. Time is short, however, and the effort is long overdue. The problem is not initially how to reduce expenditure on social services or defense. The problem is how, first of all, to redirect into useful channels all the effort and ingenuity now being spent, on the one hand, in the collection; on the other hand, in the avoidance, of tax.

7

THE AVOIDANCE OF TAX

Any scrutiny of British taxation must leave the student with a sense of wonder that Britain should have survived at all. That the country has retained or recovered a measure of prosperity is certainly a matter for surprise. It must be remembered, however, that the effects of overtaxation were not immediate in the historical examples already cited. Empires or countries strangled by their own revenue departments do not necessarily collapse at once. The process may take time and is not at first perceptible. Many an industrial or commercial business will drift on for fifty years after its initial momentum has been lost. States do the same, living on their past reputation and spending their capital reserves. Time is needed to produce a new generation, one which has been accustomed from childhood to the sense of failure. More time is needed to allow this new generation to gain high office. Even then the memory will linger for a while of past enterprise that was not merely

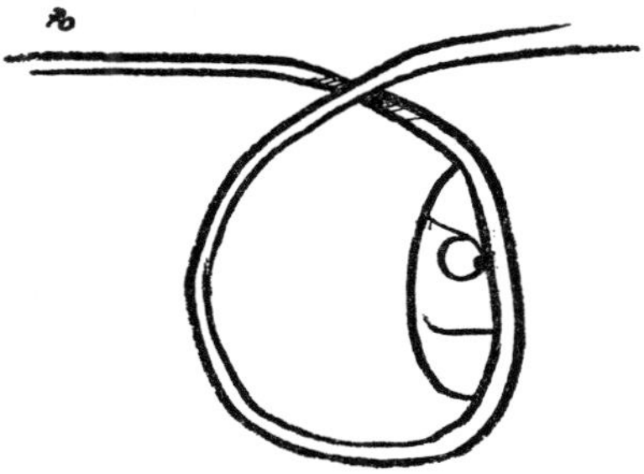

legal but honorable, of past endeavors which ended not with fiscal penalty but with public recognition. Men will look to the future even after the future has been mortgaged. To deprive them of hope takes time.

But long before that stage the combined effect of income tax and death duty should have reduced society to a dull level of financial mediocrity. Almost everyone in Britain and the United States should be living in a small suburban house with a small suburban garden, drawing a small suburban income and supporting a small suburban wife. Of parts of Australia this could almost be said to be true, and there are other countries in which this pattern of life is increasingly familiar. But there are reasons for supposing that, elsewhere, the theory still differs from the fact. Rolls-Royces and Bentleys still effortlessly overtake the other cars on the road. People still send their sons to Eton or Exeter, Groton or Rugby. At the most extravagant resorts the beaches are far from deserted; and the blue waters of the Mediterranean still reflect the sails of some quite expensive yachts. The days of financial privilege may be passing but they clearly have not passed.

Contemplation of this spectacle has produced in England the people who have come to be described as angry young men, persons whose anger may well outlast their youth. They would seem to represent a class of people whose school and university education, provided at state expense, has prepared them only for frustration. On the one hand, the Labour Party has no use for its own intellectuals, least of all those for whose education some Co-Operative Society has actually paid. On the other, the doors of privilege are still firmly closed against the products of Wigglesworth and Redbrick just as they are closed in the United States to graduates of state universities or of colleges supported by religious sects. Assured in youth that the peerage is being taxed out of existence and that the Etonian has no place in democratic society, these Redbrick graduates find that it is they themselves who have no place. Their frustration assumes literary form and they speak bitterly of the "tax dodgers" whose continued prosperity is at once mysterious and unwelcome.

Those who speak sardonically about "tax dodgers" reveal only their ignorance of the entire subject. Taxes cannot be dodged. They can be either avoided or evaded, depending upon whether the method used is legal or otherwise. Both methods are as old as taxation itself, as we have seen (on pp. 22-26 for example) and tax consultants were engaged in their "laborious and intricate work" at least as early as 1852 (see p. 44). On the subject of tax evasion a book could be written, but this is not it. Nor is it likely that a volume on that topic would be as useful as it might be voluminous. When we see booklets on How to Write a Best-Selling Novel we conclude that their authors, if they really know what they profess to teach, should be writing novels, not booklets on authorship. In the same way, an author really skilled in tax evasion would find the practice more profitable than any public explanation of the theory. So there are reasons for doubting whether a useful book on tax evasion is ever likely to appear in the bookstores. It is even a question whether a book on how to break the law might not itself be illegal.

There can be no suspicion of illegality about a book (still less, a mere chapter) on tax avoidance, but its inherent limitations must be understood. The man who has found a loophole in the law, one through which he can drive his gold-plated Cadillac, will certainly keep the secret to himself. For an individual to use the method in question may be unremarked or unopposed, but the spectacle of a whole herd converging on the same gap in the fence would invite remedial legislation, passed with a speed observable in no other kind of congressional activity. In such a chapter as this, then, the reader can expect no more than a discussion of principles, a show of historical erudition and some allusion to avoidance methods for which there would seem to be no legislative remedy.

First of all, it must be understood that the basic method of tax avoidance is today, as it has been from the beginning, to leave the country. Wealthy and distinguished men of British origin are thus to be found in Jersey, Tangier, Kenya, Bermuda, Tahiti or the Seychelles. Places of refuge for the taxpayer are territories where the tax burden is significantly less, where opportunities exist for investment or earning, and which possess a suitable agreement with Britain for the avoidance of double taxation. Territories fulfilling these basic conditions are relatively few, and of these few the majority, perhaps, have drawbacks of their own such as earthquakes, communists, cockroaches, colonial officials, centipedes, fevers, sociologists and snakes. Even the most apparently idyllic island can become the target for missionary activity or ballistic missiles. Nevertheless, this simple method of tax avoidance is open to all at the price of exile, and open to companies as well as to individuals. Much of the British merchant marine sails thus under Greek ownership and flies the brave, battle-torn ensign of Nicaragua or Panama.

For those whose business or interests, tastes or health compel them to stay in Manchester, Wellington or Montreal, the problem is not as simple. It would not be too much to say that the tax situation is apt to be complex, uncertain, obscure and confused. Amidst the obscurities there looms, however, one fundamental principle, and that is the distinction between capital and income. In the department concerned with tax collection — but in no other public department — this distinction is generally recognized. Significantly, this same distinction is observed to this extent in the United States, that long-term capital gains are taxed at no more than 25 per cent — a fact which has colored the whole complexion of the stock market, making speculation rather than investment the primary concern. The distinction is recognized for this reason, that income is subject to tax and capital subject to death duties. It is therefore the object of the tax avoider to have no income (but merely capital) while he lives, no capital (but merely income) when he dies. The tax collector's point of view is exactly

the opposite. He sees nothing but income during the victim's life and nothing but capital at his death. To reconcile these diametrically opposite views within the strained and tottering framework of the law is definitely a task for the expert. The conflict is hedged about by technicalities, the law turning out to be vague and the lawyers vaguer still. Massed formidably on the one side is the artillery of the statutes, thunderous in sound and fury but haphazard in direction. In ambush on the other side are past verdicts of the courts, almost inaudible but carefully aimed. To pass even relatively unscathed through this combined barrage and fusillade is difficult for anyone and impossible for most.

One fact apparent at the outset is that capital is more easily preserved than income. That is why the ranks of the English aristocracy have become more exclusive, perhaps, than ever before. To found a county family, complete with estates and castle, peerage and park, is now virtually impracticable. To retain the inherited position may not be easy, but it now means the maintenance of what no one else can ever have again. The social value of nobility is therefore increasing, to the annoyance of the angry young men, and even the great house is nowadays less of a burden and more of an asset. The old families are unassailably situated as compared with the new; a fact which applies to Old and New England alike. In much the same way, age generally is in a stronger position than youth. The older directors and surgeons, authors and managers, dramatists and artists mostly enjoy the advantage of having made money before 1939; or even, in some instances, before 1909. They had made their capital before taxation became ruinous. All the younger men are penalized, by contrast, for being born too late in the century.

For Englishmen with capital to preserve, the problem is not insoluble. Their first precaution must be to give everything away to their heirs by deed of gift, contriving to live thereafter for a minimum period of five years. The penalty for dying within that period is to have the gift classified as a bequest. The chief objection to this policy derives from the difficulty of knowing when the death is likely to occur. The impatient heir might see this transaction taking place when his father reaches the age of fifty-five, while the father (with whom the decision lies) might think it premature to take such a drastic step before reaching his seventieth birthday. When such a father dies at the age of seventy-four, as seems inevitable, his son and heir is all too apt to burst a blood vessel, thus incurring a second load of death duties before the first has even been assessed. Those who visit the stately homes of England are often told that the Duke is bedridden or that the Marquess's bath chair may be glimpsed on the distant terrace. They are correct in concluding, as they always do, that the Marquess died some time ago, that the bath chair contains a dummy figure and that the nobleman's body has been placed in the Frigidaire (family model) until such time as the death can be safely announced. While there may be little danger of the secret being revealed, the inconveniences involved in this type of estate-duty-avoidance are all too obvious. For one thing, the refrigerator may be wanted for something else. It is for this reason that many people prefer the alternative method of vesting the whole property in a privately owned company, which will not die.[1]

For people with capital, there are also ways of apparently foregoing income. They all work on the principle that what might, at first glance, appear to be income is really only an appreciation of capital. A method once popular was to buy and sell stocks in such a way as to avoid receiving a dividend. As most stocks rise in value before the dividend falls due, being marked down again after it has been paid, the tax avoider has had good reason to sell them before the payment and buy them back afterwards. This practice has been discouraged somewhat in England by a tax levied on the transference of stocks, as a result of which it became necessary to do rather more than buy and sell the same stock. With reasonably good advice, however, the handling of investments is not really difficult. Many types of property have been rising in value for years, some

[1] By comparison, American inheritance taxes, although even more complex, are less severe. Federal estate tax (under 1948 Revenue Act) starts with 3 per cent on estates of $60,000 and rises to 61 per cent on an estate of $50,000,000. Even at the equivalent of about $2,000,000, British death duties would amount to 75 per cent. As against that, there are state inheritance taxes in addition and these vary from state to state.

city real estate being a case in point. Great gains involve appreciable risks but a steady and inconspicuous capital appreciation is fairly easy to arrange.

While taxable unearned income can thus be minimized, it is usually unwise to deny having any income at all. Income there must be, but kept under rigid control by the formation, or (even better) the acquisition of an incorporated company. A company formed for purposes of tax avoidance is usually agricultural in character and associated with some singularly unproductive acreage of land. Such profits as may arise from the other activities of the company are offset by losses on the farm. These losses arise in two ways. In the first place, it is overstaffed and overequipped, the cook and the governess counting as dairymaids, the station wagon and jeep being classed as agricultural implements and their gasoline consumption placed to the credit of some rarely operated tractor. In the second place, the farm's salable production in poultry, eggs, milk and fruit will prove a perpetual disappointment to all concerned. In so far as there is any profit from the company's total activities, it will be neatly swallowed up by directors' fees, which will admittedly be subject to tax but only as earned income and as distributed, moreover, among several closely related members of the Board.

The company which has been acquired rather than formed works on a different principle. In the taxation of companies, the tax collector looks to an average result over a number of years, allowing the profits of one year to be set against the losses of the years that are past. It follows that a company which has seen nothing but disaster and which is worthless to its proprietors may be quite valuable to someone else. Its past losses can be advertised as an asset

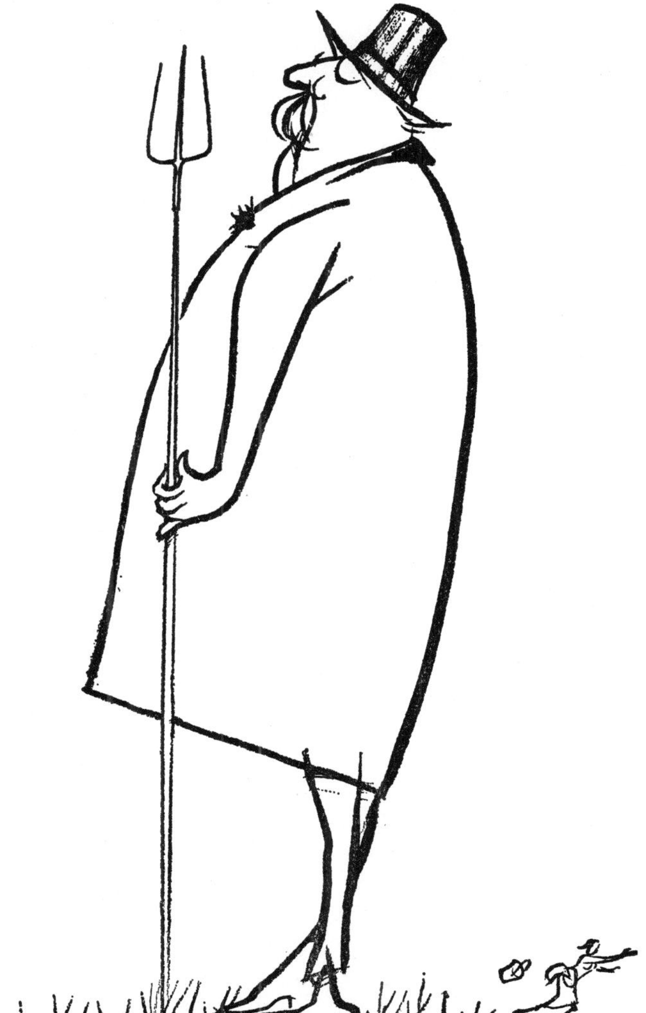

for sale, as something to offset future gains, and this is often done. The danger arises when the guaranteed loss turns out to include outstanding and undisclosed liabilities. Whether business enterprises are actually started for this purpose would be an interesting subject for inquiry. Tropically situated governments have sometimes offered a reward for the destruction of venomous snakes, usually on the basis of length, only to discover that the snakes were being bred for purposes of claiming the reward. In much the same way, unsuccessful businesses, like antique furniture and vintage cars, may have to be manufactured. If we hear, therefore, of companies promoted for the sale of woolen underwear in equatorial Africa, or for the distribution of ice cream in Lapland, we can fairly suspect that some such scheme has been launched.

One way and another, the person with capital can, by ceaseless effort and considerable ingenuity, preserve what he already has. In point of fact, however, the possessors of capital are often widows and orphans, people whose forebears have done worthy service and the crippled veterans of past campaigns in Flanders or Matabeleland. These will ordinarily lose whatever they possess, their capital dwindling by the normal processes of inflation. Their losses are avoidable, to be sure, but only by a constant study of the *Financial Times* and by continual contact with the market. This alertness in matters of investment is a quality which relatively few of them possess. Some are too young, others too old, and the rest too obsessed with their gardens and dogs. By an inevitable process, they will mostly end with nothing.

If we turn now to consider the position of those without capital, we must remark that their plight is infinitely worse. To rise by legal means and enter the ranks of the socially privileged (except by marriage) is impracticable for all but a very few. To accumulate capital implies just such an excess of income over expenditure as the tax system seems designed to prevent. In many professions the young man makes little, the higher earnings being the reward for persistence in middle age. No allowance is made for this long apprenticeship, the income being fully taxed as soon as it becomes appreciable. Even the moderately successful lawyer, when he has paid for his children's education and provided for his own old age, will be fortunate indeed to have much surplus. There is only one privileged profession in this respect, and that is the Civil Service. No other career offers such financial reward at so early an age, with status and pension and nothing to lose.

When all the difficulties have been sufficiently emphasized, the fact remains that the feat of achieving financial independence is still occasionally performed by legal means. For the purpose of investigating how this is done we must ignore, from the outset, the winners of Sweepstakes and professional entertainers such as Hollywood stars and baseball players. They may be and doubtless are an important new class in the classless society, but it would be unhelpful to urge the reader to join their ranks. To utter the advice "Win the Irish Sweepstake" is no more useful than to say "Be born the heir to the sixteenth Earl of Pembroke and Montgomery." What is desirable is not always within reach. Our study must be confined rather to what is immediately feasible, and for this purpose we must return to first principles. Our concern is now solely with income, and we have seen already that income cannot escape taxation. So the problem is how legally to become more prosperous without receiving income, thus building up such a surplus as may be described, in the end, as capital. A little reflection will show that the desired result can be achieved in two ways, and most readily in fact by a combination of both. First, the income must be received, for the most part, in kind. Second, against the income in cash there must be set an equivalent and legally deductible loss.

In theory, and sometimes in practice, the most successful exponent of income avoidance is the subsistence farmer. What he makes is almost impossible to discover and what he loses will prove to be his almost sole topic of conversation. But what is possible for the true son of the soil is by no means as easy for anyone else. For the retired brigadier or colonel, the likelihood is that his losses will be real and his income not theoretically but actually negative. The better policy is to engage not in agriculture but in business. The businessman can so arrange matters that his travel expenses, his entertainment of friends, his car and his flat, his wife and his daughter are all provided for at the firm's expense. For tax purposes the only vehicle is a van, the flat an office, the wife a secretary and the daughter a copy typist, all travels are for promoting trade and all restaurant bills incurred while regaling clients. This largesse is as useful to the company as to the man it employs, for it all goes to reduce the tax payable on its profits (see p. 88).

With the tax avoider's income thus reduced to an insignificant figure, his next step is to extinguish that small total by an assumed burden of insurance premiums, annuities, mortgages and trusts. With but average ingenuity an income can be made to vanish like the Cheshire Cat, leaving nothing behind but a self-satisfied grin, not strictly speaking liable to assessment. And a concealed income can gradually turn into capital. Remember, however, that the tax avoider must go soberly about his business, keeping his real expenses to the minimum. Observe too that his success in gaining prosperity will be due as much to his economy as to his skill in tax avoidance. To acquire capital, the basic method (apart from marrying money or gambling) is to limit expenditure while expanding income. To this policy a masterly avoidance of tax is essential but auxiliary. It is not in itself the key to success.

One other word of warning must be uttered. The above-mentioned methods of tax avoidance are legal in theory but may well be challenged in practice. That the car is vital to the business may be more or less true, but the extent to which it is privately used could be matter for argument. There might be dispute again about the secretary's travel expenses or the rent of the flat. Once your claim became the subject of litigation, the result would be a matter of chance. That being so, the safe rule is always to have as much money available as if the most pessimistic forecasts were sure to prove uniformly correct. For there can be nothing more fatal than to be in the tax collector's debt. By professing inability to pay at the time of demand, you make it virtually impossible to pay at all. When you produce the money, there is inevitably the question as to how you acquired it. If earned — and you can hardly claim that it was stolen — the sum paid is itself liable to tax. That new demand can be satisfied only by another payment, which is itself taxable; and so on indefinitely. It is by this chain of events that many a tax avoider is brought to ruin. We hear thus of one film actor who dare not set foot in the United States, of a novelist permanently exiled from Britain, of other people who slink round in dark spectacles and false beards, and of others again whose beards are genuine. Some distinguished people can escape from the toils only by bankruptcy or suicide. These clearly provide us with

examples of a sort of policy we should do well to reject. The avoidance of tax demands, it is clear, a business acumen of the highest order.

While it is thus proper to emphasize that taxation can thus be avoided by the astute and worldly, we must also remember that many heirs to property are neither worldly nor astute. They include widows and orphans, brigadiers and wing commanders, horse lovers, dog breeders, professors, and poets. People of this sort will often lack the business sense which alone could save them. Nor is this any matter for wonder. To survive in the jungle of tax ridden finance, the classical scholar or horticulturalist would have to become a businessman, exchanging the lexicon or seed catalogue for the market letter and prices current. Such a transformation is more feasible than might be supposed but brings with it a heavier penalty than many feel able to bear. The man who can save his rose garden only by devoting his energies to finance may fairly object that the rose garden, when saved, will no longer be his. In theory, the estate of an absent-minded philologist can be handled for him by a man of affairs. In practice, absence of mind will soon lead to absence of income. For businessmen it is relatively easy to buy from each other at a discount, enjoying an invisible income which is free of tax. But the scholar who attempts to do the same, and who succeeds, will no longer be a scholar. By saving his property he will have lost all reason for his existence. Many prefer to live their own chosen lives for as long as they can, sacrificing their financial independence rather than discarding, much sooner, their personal freedom. For people like these, the time will come when their old home must be sold.

This moment in a family's history is marked by the appearance of a notice on the gate. FOR SALE it reads and the description follows of so many acres and so many rooms. "Suitable" pleads the auctioneer, "for school or similar institution." The truth is that it is often suitable for nothing. But there is a special vocabulary for use on these occasions. "Imposing" means Victorian Gothic, and "Quaint" means derelict. "Tudor replica" means something dreadful, and "In need of repair" means on the point of collapse. Some houses are really suitable, of course, for an institutional purpose. Of one such house, adapted as a Home for Difficult Boys, the older neighbors could remark sourly that it had never been anything else. In general, whatever its ultimate use, the house is sold for a fraction of the sum it cost to build.

FOR SALE says the placard and the passer-by notices the leaves drifting over the ill-kept drive. It is November and those who have attended the auction of the furniture walk briskly through the gathering dusk. "I just went to see inside," says one. "I meant to bid for the kitchen dresser," replies her friend, "but Tom tells me that it has woodworm." They step aside as the last furniture van lurches through the lodge gates. Standing between the Ionic columns of the doorway, the owner (or he who until yesterday was owner) hears the dwindling sound of the van's departure, and then turns to face the cold and empty hall. Somewhere in the kitchen wing a crate is being nailed up. The hammer blows echo faintly down the corridor. All else is silent now, save for the footsteps of the recent squire. Patches of dirt show where stood the heavy pieces of furniture, which latterly were never moved. The smell of dry rot is quite unmistakable now, and the light from murky windows falls dimly on the dusty floor. It is strange how suddenly a household is brought to nothing. Up to a few days since, all looked as it had always looked, faded perhaps but still the family home. But the curtains, when shifted, were found to be moth-eaten and worthless, the carpets worn out but with the bare patch hidden until then by the settee. The china had its chipped side to the wall and the prints were spoiled by mildew and decay. Even Grandfather's sword, which hung over the fireplace, was found, on moving, to be rusted in its sheath.

The hammering has finished now and the squire's footsteps echo through the empty house. Here is the room where he himself was born, and there the room where Great-aunt Mabel died. This was the nursery once — but whose was that, the room adjacent and for long disused? Poor cousin Rachel's? Or Dick's when home from school? Who is now to know, and who would care? That life is over. Now begins the awkward slow descent. Here hung Grandmother's portrait on the stair, and here is the banister down which the children slid. Here was the relic from Gettysburg and there the oar blade with the College arms. At the stair's foot there used to be that painting of Leonidas, that won the steeplechase in '93. The last tread creaks and here's the hall. There's darkness now and quiet, save the door, which, closing softly, leaves the house asleep . . .

For ordinary people who want to preserve their houses and property, the tragedy of taxation carried to its present lengths is that ingenuity and energy are being deflected into the wrong channels. While this book is in no sense a guide to tax evasion or even a commentary on the methods of tax evasion now in use, the reader can rest assured that taxes are evaded and that on a considerable scale. People who would describe themselves as law-abiding citizens, people who would unhesitatingly assist the police during a riot, people who have served their country in war and peace, will readily falsify a tax return if they feel that this can be done with safety. They know that skillful evasion is more rewarding than any addition to their taxable income. They feel that the taxes are fixed on a penal scale by the votes of those whose own contribution will be small. They conclude that evasion is not only profitable but justified. It is this belief that transfers them, by gradual stages, from the ranks of the law-abiding to the ranks of the rebellious. Once a man has become accustomed to evading taxation, once he has come to regard the policeman as a possible danger and not as an ally, he will begin to show less

respect for any kind of law. In the days of prohibition the smuggler of liquor ended as a murderer. From breaking a law which everyone could see to be senseless he went on to break every other law there was. On a smaller scale, the tax laws are having something like the same effect.

For those whose normal activities are illegal there is something peculiarly unfair in the additional penalty which may be imposed for a tax offense. For an accurate return would be such a damaging confession as no one should be compelled to make. Without attempting to justify the activities of gangsters, the impartial student must sympathize, up to a point, with their predicament. Nor can he regard their prosecution with the satisfaction he is supposed to register. For the attitude of the tax authorities is typically unreasonable. What sort of returns do they expect the criminal to file? Place Form 1040 before an American hoodlum and you put the man in a very difficult position. Assuming him to be as strictly truthful as Congress expects him to be, his return will be something like this:

FORM 1040 U.S. INDIVIDUAL INCOME TAX RETURN	FOR CALENDAR YEAR 1960		1960
	Please type or print plainly		Do not write in these spaces
	Name:	*JOE PLUGUGLY*	
	Home Address:	*C/o Mike's Bar, Fourth Avenue, New York, N.Y.*	Serial No.
	Occupation:	*Stick-up & Snatch Racket*	Cashier's stamp

So far there has only been slight embarrassment and someone has restrained Joe from affixing the Cashier's stamp, which would have been easy for him (he collects them, actually). Come now, however, to Section 2.

2. Enter your total wages, salaries, bonuses, commissions and other compensation received in 1960, before payroll deductions. Persons claiming traveling, transportation or reimbursed expenses, and Outside Salesmen, see instructions.

A. Employer's name	B. Where employed	C. Total wages	D. Tax withheld
		$	$
3. Less excludable portion			
4. Balance (Item 2 less Item 3) 5. If you received dividends, interest or any other income (or loss) give details on page 2. Enter total here —			
6. Adjusted Gross Income — Enter Total here —			

Confronted by this, Joe realizes that he has had no wages, salaries or bonuses — grossly unfair as this may seem — his gains being best defined perhaps as "other compensation." As against these gains he can certainly claim traveling and other expenses. Under "Employer's name" Joe writes "None." Under "Where employed" he writes "At different addresses in New York State." Under "Total wages" he writes "$17,000" and under "Tax withheld" he writes "Nil." To arrive at the figure of $17,000 Joe has deducted:

(a) All his meal and lodging costs when on temporary assignment.
(b) Cost and maintenance of blowtorch, drill, crowbar and other equipment *genuinely* essential to his business.
(c) Cost of providing and maintaining various costumes *genuinely* necessary to his business (including police uniform and robes of Supreme Court Judge).

Section 3 does not apply to him, so Joe's Balance is the same as his return under Section 2. Come now, therefore, to Section 5. Joe has received no dividends but he can claim a loss through inability to attend to his business during the first two months of the year; a period during which he was in prison. But what about "any other income"? Joe derives a subsidiary income from protection money, blackmail and cheating at cards, as against which he can claim for bribing the police, for remuneration of accomplices and for entertaining victims. But the whole matter is complicated and difficult to explain. Joe gives up the task in despair, knowing that he is expected to complete his return "under the penalties of perjury." For him to file an honest return is scarcely possible.

Yet another difficulty is that of security. We know that the Internal Revenue Service is supposed to treat all tax returns as strictly confidential, but is this a secrecy upon which the gangster can rely? If we study the case history of the Lindbergh kidnaping in 1932 we find examples of Intelligence Unit Agents actually *working* with the police. How are we to know that this co-operation is not the normal thing? Until there is some definite and public assurance on this point we cannot expect criminals to confide freely in the Internal Revenue Service. In the meanwhile, with things deliberately made difficult for them, many criminals are likely to go on making returns which are misleading in detail and inaccurate in their statement of total liability, while criminals who are incapable of falsehood will refrain as hitherto from filing any tax return at all. And who shall blame them? What is obviously needed is a special form to meet the needs of special taxpayers. In rough outline it should be like this:

FORM 1040(Z)	For Calendar Year 1960 — Secret	1960
U.S. INDIVIDUAL INCOME TAX RETURN FOR THOSE WHOSE ACTIVITIES ARE MAINLY (1) ILLEGAL	Please write in invisible ink and on the undertaking that the form will be destroyed within two days of receipt.	Do not write in these spaces
	Present Alias:	Serial No.
	Accommodation Address:	Cashier's stamp

(1) Persons whose activities are illegal only to a lesser degree and whose chief sources of income are more or less legitimate should obtain Substitute Form 1040(Y) in which provision is made for their special case. For a definition of activities which are deemed to be mainly illegal, see *Instructions.*

With this amount of special consideration, there can be no doubt that many criminals would be proud to contribute to their country's revenue. Even if some checks received should prove impossible to negotiate, and even if some cash turned out to be counterfeit, the experiment would be at least as noble as some other experiments the United States has known.

To turn to the predicament of the great majority, it is obvious that some otherwise law-abiding people would evade taxes in any case. Their number would be small, however, if their margin of profit were less. With a tax of about 10 per cent of income, the cost of evasion (or even of avoidance) becomes for most people more than the amount of the tax. Even with tax at 20 per cent, the skill now devoted to evading the tax might be more profitably directed toward increasing the income. And, given anything like an even choice, the average citizen would rather give his money to the state than to a group of lawyers, accountants, advisers and experts. It is less trouble, for one thing, and he may feel generally sympathetic toward many of the objects in view. It is the widening of the gap between the cost of evasion and the far higher cost of the tax that tends, eventually, to make criminals out of honest men. In many parts of Britain people overestimate the strength of the law. They feel that the forces of civilization are absolutely in the ascendant and have little to fear from subversion or crime. Those who have lived in, say, Liverpool, have no such illusions. They realize that civilization is precarious and widely in abeyance after sunset. They know, as others cannot, that with the battle so evenly matched, we cannot afford to drive even wavering adherents into the enemy's camp.

While the whole question of tax avoidance and evasion must hinge on the ratio between the cost of avoidance (or evasion) and the amount of the tax, there is one other factor of which little notice has been taken. The taxpayer's reluctance to pay has been strengthened in recent years by his growing conviction that the money he pays will be largely wasted. This was not true to the same extent in former ages. The earliest rulers of civilized states might be guilty, at times, of personal extravagance, but this is not to be confused with waste in the modern sense. It could not be said of palaces, pleasure grounds, costly robes, dancing girls, concubines, elaborate food and rare wine that they were exactly wasted. They might be consumed, they might be discarded; but what else, after all, is anyone to do with them? Insufficient use of the facilities available would certainly have been wasteful. But it is not, in the main, a story of such neglect that history has to tell; nor, incidentally, would the taxpayer of the ancient world have been particularly pleased by a display of economy at court. He would share in fabulous pleasures to the extent of hearing them described, and for any but the most meanly envious there is a satisfaction in vicarious luxury which is not to be derived from a tale of thrift. Kings could economize, to be sure, over the dancing girls' attire, and often seem to have done so; but parsimonious rulers were never loved and even those merely luxurious were felt to be serving a purpose of some kind.

In modern times there has been relatively little extravagance of this picturesque sort; so little, indeed, that Adam Smith, for one, scarcely mentions its possible effect. In laying down principles of taxation, he emphasized equality of incidence, certainty in method, convenience of form and economy in collection. He saw less reason to insist that the sums collected should not be too obviously thrown away. But that nowadays is becoming a principal point at issue. In place of the expenses which used to arise from what a few would regard as extravagance we now have far heavier expenses arising from what everyone can see to be futile. The wastefulness of government is thus becoming a major factor in the situation. It is one thing to pay taxes for objects which all must agree to be necessary. It is quite another to pay for what is needless, harmful or absurd. The subject of tax avoidance thus leads inevitably to the subject of waste.

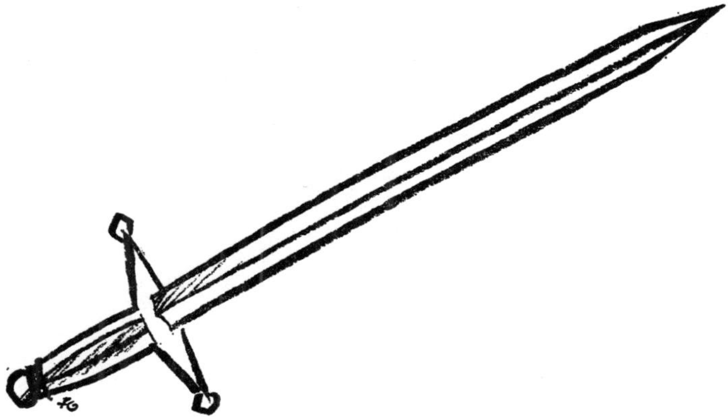

8

WASTEFUL WAR

WASTE, like taxation itself, has its origin in war. Men whose expectation of life is short have their own outlook where expenditure is concerned. The sailor who fires a torpedo, the gunner who demolishes the building which masks his field of fire, the airman who bales out from his four-engined bomber cannot worry too much about the cost. Economy ceases to be relevant for those who may never foot the bill. Destruction may be wasteful but destruction is war. So it is natural to burn the piano as firewood, so that those may be warm tonight who may never live to see the day. This cheerful disregard of property and expense begins on the battlefield itself but spreads back along the supply lines, reaches railhead, crosses the sea, and so comes at last to Whitehall or the Pentagon. There it mingles with extravagance of quite another kind: that extravagance in staffing to which the present author drew attention in a previous book.

It would be quite wrong, of course, to imagine that staff accumulation is a new problem. There exists in the British Museum a plaintive letter written on papyrus in A.D. 288, signed by Servaeus Africanus, addressed to the district governors of Middle Egypt and reading as follows:

> It is apparent from the accounts alone that a number of persons wishing to batten on the estates of the Treasury have invented titles for themselves such as controllers, secretaries or superintendents, whereby they procure no advantage to the Treasury but swallow up the profits. (Papyrus 752)

That is the problem in a nutshell and the noble Roman's description is one we need not seek to better. Among the warriors of Whitehall there is something of the wastefulness of war and much of the overstaffing which seems endemic to their vicinity. All this has been known elsewhere and before. What is more peculiar to Britain and the United States is the way in which vast peacetime expenditure on the armed forces can leave a country totally unprepared for war. This is the more remarkable in Britain, where the population is more warlike in character than foreign rulers tend to believe. Britain presents, in fact, an extraordinary contrast between governmental ineptitude and habitual success.

To begin with, the British are probably better at fighting than at anything else, displaying on many (though not on all) occasions of peril a useful combination of resolution, tenacity, enterprise and resource. These virtues are associated, moreover, with that capacity for idleness which

warriors so frequently reveal. It is the more remarkable, therefore, that British preparations for war should be as ineffective as they have often proved to be. The governmental tendency in these matters is to prepare, as we know, for the last war but one. Thus, the years immediately preceding World War II were devoted by the British Army to a training which would undoubtedly have won us the Boer War had that conflict been in the future rather than in the past. Troops were cunningly clad in a uniform which blended imperceptibly with the veldt or indeed with the Khyber Pass, their presence being betrayed only by the brilliant polish on their leatherwork and brass. On training exercises the officers were mounted and the vehicles largely horse-drawn. When the enemy was encountered, his fire realistically indicated by waving flags, the accepted practice was for the commanding officer to canter on his white charger to the summit of some convenient hill, followed by his adjutant and intelligence officer. Lowering his binoculars, he would say "Theah's the enemy!" He would presently be joined on the skyline by his company commanders, also on horseback and waving their maps. The commanding officer would then issue his orders for battle: "You, Carruthers, will attack up *theah*, and you, Willoughby, will be in reserve *heah*," and his officers would canter away to their respective tasks. There were those who expressed occasional doubt as to whether horses would really figure as prominently as this in the next war, since they had actually played little part in the last, but this heresy was very properly frowned upon. Nor did it find favor in the United States, where the Field Artillery of World War II was trained on horse-drawn guns originally designed (as the French 75mm.) for the Franco-

Prussian War, and where the aspiring gunner officer had still to master the Science of Hippology.

Defenders of this traditional pattern of maneuver explain that to train or equip oneself for the next war is not really feasible. The British plan, they insist, is to wait for the war to begin, inspect the conflict in progress and then begin to decide upon the sort of equipment that might be useful. It is argued in defense of this technique, which admittedly involves heavy casualties at the outset, that the enemy, being the aggressor, knows when the war will begin and can arm himself accordingly. To be continually ready for any possible war would be prohibitively expensive, so we might just as well defer the whole question of weapons until we know whom we are to fight and where. Is it to be tropical kit or skis? Best to economize by having neither. Concentrate, in the meanwhile, on *esprit de corps*, on morale and on playing the game. These moral qualities, it is argued, are both useful and cheap. We are sure to win in any case because, as our school textbooks made clear, we always do.

There would be something in this argument for peacetime economy if it were only based on fact. The sad reality is that British war expenditure in times of peace has been considerable and that opponents better equipped for war have spent far less on their weapons than we have chosen to suppose. This is especially true of Germany prior to World War II. It has now been shown that any picture we may have of a German industry geared to war in 1939 is entirely false. More than that, we know that the Germany of 1943 was still not particularly geared to war. When Hamburg was largely flattened or burned by the Royal Air Force the effect was to improve German war

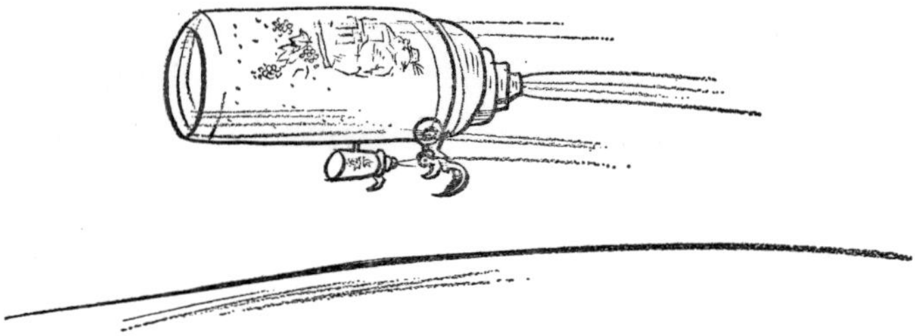

production. Many craftsmen were forced to enter munition factories whose previous efforts had been in manufacturing (say) ornamental earthenware beer mugs, but whose place of work had been destroyed. The real contrast is not between two levels of peacetime expenditure on future war but between the opposite ways in which the money was spent. The Germans spent their money on tanks and guns, largely purchased from privately owned armament firms. The British spent a comparable sum upon a vast officialdom and a huge technocracy. Of the civilian administrative burden carried by the armed services much could be said and something has been written. It is enough to remark for the moment, however, that there is also a uniformed bureaucracy and one equally incapable of deployment against the enemy. The cost of all this paperwork absorbed the money which might have been spent on artillery and anti-tank weapons. Much of the money voted added nothing to our strength.

This last point merits some detailed attention. We were all told in youth that the Germans began World War I after years of careful preparation, catching the British typically unready, no thought of war having so much as entered their minds. This picture is not entirely accurate. The sad fact is that the British had spent more money on their forces than had the Germans but with remarkably little result. The expenditure figures for 1911, for example, read as follows:

	Army	Navy	Total
British	£27,760,300	£40,603,700	£68,364,000
German	£39,930,100	£22,431,000	£62,361,100

The result of this different emphasis in allocation was to give Britain a narrow margin of superiority at sea and a quite startling inferiority on land. On the basis of cost the British army might have been outnumbered, and inevitably, in the ratio of about 10 to 7. Its actual inferiority was out of all proportion. British strength in 1911 was reckoned at 254,000 regular soldiers together with what W. R. Lawson calls "a wavering fringe of Territorials." The peace strength of the German Army, which had cost *less* than the British in 1903, came to 622,000 men. When war began in 1914 the Germans put 98 divisions into the field (11 Cavalry and 87 Infantry). The British could muster 7 divisions (1 Cavalry and 6 Infantry) with 14 Territorial divisions still below establishment and still but partly trained. Allowing that the German Landwehr troops were no better, and allowing that British troops in garrisons overseas might equal another 6 divisions (1 Cavalry, 5 Infantry), that still leaves the German Army with a superiority of 98 to 27 in formations and 4,400,000 to 417,000 in men. It admittedly cost more money, but not in *that* proportion. And the Germans were opposing their machine guns to British rifles. The British admittedly knew more about warfare than either their opponents or allies (having been at war more recently) but in every other respect they were outclassed. They had voted the money but that was nearly all they had done. Funds had been frittered away on correspondence and printing, upon clerks and ink. The British system of accounting was in itself worth an army corps to the other side; as indeed it still is.

World War I having taught the British nothing, they entered World War II with the same disparity of forces and with the same sort of comparison in expense. As the German government published no military statistics after Hitler took office, an estimate of its expenditure can be no more than guesswork. Such guesses as have been made, however, would allow Germany a military expenditure of £1333 million in 1938, compared with the known British expenditure of £391 million. With this not inconsiderable sum the British were unable to equal their 1914 record. Instead of 7 divisions in the field, they could now provide only 4, with another 5 devoted to anti-aircraft defense and 13 Territorial divisions, which were later officially made to number 26. On the most optimistic reckoning, this would imply a total of 22 divisions, mostly ill trained and all ill equipped, but more or less present and numbered off. By a comparison in relative expense the Germans, spending over three times as much, should have put, say, 75 divisions in the field. Instead they were able to mobilize 105 divisions, six of them armored and four of them motorized.

There is no reason to suppose that the postwar ratio between expense and result is any better and there are reasons for supposing that it is probably worse. Nor is the wastage confined to the army, nor for that matter to Britain. The Royal Navy employs a body of people of whom 60 per cent (1958) turn out to be civilians. These civilians number vastly more than they did before World War II, when a far larger fleet was maintained, and their total number is not even shown in the Navy Estimates. In maintaining this total, trade union rules play an important part. Only a shipwright can paint a flagpole! At the Admiralty itself, there are 6000 more civilians employed than in 1933. Altogether, of 300,000 people on the payroll, only 15 per cent are in seagoing ships, so that there are five ashore for every man afloat. As a matter of comparison the Army of the United States employs no fewer than 1,180,000 civilians, a total which would be formidable in-

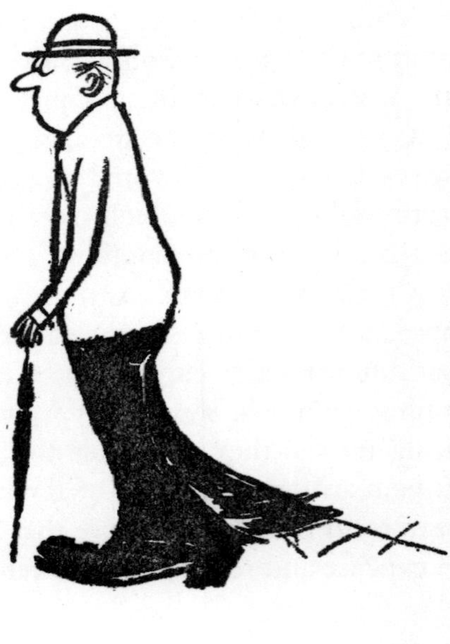

deed if wars were to be won by sheer weight of correspondence.

So far this chapter has been devoted mainly to British waste connected with war, not because the British are peculiarly wasteful but because the United States figures for waste soar beyond comprehension. Of every $100 collected in federal income tax it has been calculated, by Senator Bridges, that $59.50 goes in Defense, $10.50 toward interest on Federal Debt (mainly the result of war) and $6.60 for Veterans. And these defense costs have done much to increase federal expenditure which, taking 20 per cent of the gross national product ($85 billion) in 1938, took 26 per cent of the gross national product ($440 billion) in 1957. It was also World War II which left the federal government operating 700 large and 19,000 smaller businesses, losing between them almost $1 billion a month. With one citizen out of five on the government payroll, we must expect extravagance; but hardly the extravagance which we actually find where defense is concerned.

One is familiar with the process by which blue-prints are prepared for a scheme which has finally to be scrapped. No good, is the final verdict. We must try something else. This sort of thing is inevitable in times like the present. What is startling, however, is the amount spent before the No good verdict is expressed. In 1958 the Pentagon is supposed to have written off $7.5 billion in surplus equipment. The Navy expenses include $68 million for aircraft engines — not wanted; $78 million for the Regulus A.A. Missile — abandoned; and $200 million for an experiment with seaplanes — which failed. Not to be outdone, the Air Force puts in items like these: $60 million in spare parts for the F.100 Fighter — unwanted; $70 million for the

Goose Missile — given up; $374 million for the air-to-air Rascal — abandoned; and $750 million for the Navaho guided missile — scrapped. Would it not have paid to do the thinking first and spend the money afterwards? But that is not the government way. If the dollars are there (and they are) — spend them! When we turn from these statistics to find that the Joint Chiefs of Staff need 400 more staff with 31 instead of 13 Under and Assistant Secretaries; 70,000 square feet of additional floor space, and alterations, with furniture, costing $350,000, we feel that these expenses are negligible; as, by comparison, they are. Stunned by the tale of thousands of millions wasted, how should the taxpayers worry about the cost of legal subsections in Defense (and other) Departments which do nothing but apply to the Patent Office for patents which the U.S. Government issues to itself for no discoverable purpose? Who are they to complain that an Air Force bill for $13.94, payable by a former employee, should have attached to it a 28-page invoice with the signatures of two lieutenant-colonels, three majors, one captain, a first-lieutenant and thirteen civilian department heads? Who are they to complain and what purpose would be served by their complaint? They are merely the folk who must pay the bill.

The wastefulness of officialdom is generally known but the size of the technocracy has tended to escape notice. It has also been assumed that technical experts serve a purpose even if administrators do not. A more careful scrutiny of the facts would reveal the truth that an army of technocrats in Britain has served mainly as an obstacle to progress. The inventions and ideas have come from regimental officers or from engineers employed in industry. All that the technocrats have done is to find reasons why some newly invented weapon shall be rejected as useless. From the harebrained character of some weapons they did choose to accept we might infer that the term "lunatic" would fitly apply to all they turned down. This conclusion would, unfortunately, be false. When von Rundstedt's tanks went through the Polish armies in 1939 the designer of the P.I.A.T. (invented in 1937) was sitting, metaphorically, on the doorstep of the British War Office, vainly trying to interest officialdom in the weapon that could have stopped the German blitzkrieg at the outset. Nor was this an isolated instance of official obduracy, for the best weapons of the past seem to have come from anywhere but the royal arsenals.

The culverins used against the Spanish Armada were the handiwork of Sussex gunfounders. Marlborough's infantry carried small arms made by Brooke's of Birmingham. Wellington's riflemen were equipped with Ezekiel Baker's rifle, his artillery supplied with the case shot invented by Lieutenant Shrapnel. With the reign of Victoria, however, the official ramparts were raised higher and the inventor's life became one of frustration. Men like Metford, Mills, Stokes, Pomeroy, Lewis, Le Mesurier, Burney, and Blacker struggled mostly in vain. The result has been well described by the last of these, who says that our present tanks are those we should have had in 1937, that our field artillery of 1939 was just what we had needed in 1914, our field gun of 1914 would have been just a trifle better than the enemy's Nordenfeldts at Colenso in 1899, while our 15-pounders used in South Africa might just possibly have outmatched the Afghan field artillery at Maiward in 1878.[1] The strangest aspect of this saga is the way

[1] See article by Lt. Colonel L. V. S. Blacker in the *Army Quarterly*, October, 1957.

in which British armies have found themselves inferior in weapons not merely to such technically proficient people as the French or the Germans but to folk who had improvised their weapons on the eve of battle. We thus suffered more casualties than we should from the Lancaster rifles of Yankee insurgents, from the homemade rifles of Afghan tribesmen, from the Fuzzy-Wuzzy small arms, and even from the submachine guns of the I.R.A.

Our official military technocracy, we should be better without. The best equipment has been conceived, designed and produced by private firms rather than public arsenals. As for the official scientists, they would do better work with B.S.A. or Vickers-Armstrong. The latter firm had by 1928 given Britain the best tanks in the world. At a later period, and one of real crisis, the position was saved not by our own technocrats but by Chrysler Motors Corporation of Detroit, as also by the Browning family of Utah. Now, in 1959, the British infantryman is being issued with an automatic rifle, not from Woolwich but from Belgium, and this takes place twenty years after the Americans adopted the Garand and forty years after the Mexican infantry were issued with the Mondragon, made in Switzerland. From the beginning, the best small arms have been made for the sportsman and the military technocrat has limped painfully behind.

It would be serious enough if the result of our system was merely to be measured by the obsolescence of our weapons. But there is also the appalling waste involved in the complexities of design and the multiplication of parts. A very few years ago it was remarked that plugs, F.H., for shells and bombs, used literally by the million, were made according to over two hundred different specifications and sizes and in material varying from cast iron to plastic, whereas they might have been standardized for each diameter required. Quite recently all the central heating pipes at one base (R.A.F.) were replaced, not because they were worn out (and in fact they were not) but because they were twenty years old and this was their official "life." Nor is the situation bettered by the use of an antiquated system of cost accounting, to which the army reverted after a far better system had been actually in operation.

Real economy has been very properly defined by the late Elbert Hubbard as the exact opposite of mere saving and stinting and doing without. "It means the prevention of waste, the conservation of all the valuable energies and materials and the abolition of muddle." This is true, but we have to observe that we nowadays add to the old waste through complexity and muddle a new kind of waste which has been steadily growing since about 1924. It is typified by the story told of a certain Minister for War, whose identity can be suitably concealed under the purely imaginary name of Waugh-Bellona. Asking a certain N.C.O. whether his men had all they needed, the Minister was told that they were short of magazines. Shocked at this tale of hardship, the Minister began to discuss the supply of periodicals, little realizing that the sergeant was referring to the magazines used with a light automatic. The tendency here exemplified is the provision of luxuries instead of weapons. The sergeant in question may later have been killed in action for lack of an anti-tank weapon. He may have lived that day to wrestle, later still, with smith guns and hispano cannon. But in neither case would he have been much consoled by issues of *Country Life* and *Sphere*.

So far from being reversed, this habit is now intensified. The warship of today is insulated with Fiberglas, decked with shock-cushioned plastic and decorated in pastel shades chosen by a psychologist as restful to the eye. Washrooms are tiled with porcelain and bunks are paneled in fumed oak. From the newspaper description the reader is left in doubt as to whether guns are mounted or not. That they are is merely to be inferred from a sailor's comment that the ratings will be able to sleep through a battle. But for this one reference the casual reader of the daily press might be forgiven for supposing that the purpose of our newest warships is purely recreational. Whether the ordinary seaman attracted to the Service by promises of security and comfort is exactly the man we want is for the expert to decide. But we shall be ill served by our navy if the cost of interior decoration is met by economizing in practice ammunition or merely by having fewer ships in commission. An inner-spring mattress is of only limited use to the sailor whose squadron is outnumbered, outgunned and outfought.

What is disheartening about the history of naval and military administration is that real attempts to economize usually end in additional expense. It is true that there was a significant reduction in the estimates between 1860 and 1871, but Lord Randolph Churchill's great effort in 1887 followed a pattern which has since become the norm. He called attention to the appalling waste of money in the armed services, showing how little of it was spent to any purpose. He pointed out that the fortresses were untenable, the artillery obsolete, the rifles defective, the bayonets fragile, the warships ill designed and the naval guns liable to burst even when fired with a reduced charge. The

Osborn

Admiralty, he proved, exported Australian tinned meat to Australia, rum to Jamaica and rice to India. One branch of the War Office cost £5000 a year and had as its function the supervising of an annual expenditure which amounted to £250. The estimates, he was able to show, were framed in such a manner as to leave Parliament without the smallest idea of what the services cost; and the expense had in fact increased by millions. But what began as a demand for reduction in expenditure was transformed inevitably into a demand for greater efficiency. According to Sir Winston Churchill, this always happens.

> The Government and their official advisers at the proper moment now shift their ground with an adroitness of past experience. They admit the damaging facts which can no longer be denied. The politicians explain that they arise from the neglect or incapacity of their predecessors. They recognise the public demand for more perfect instruments of war. They declare that they will not flinch from their plain duty (whatever others may have done); they will repair the deficiencies which clearly exist; they will correct the abuses which have been exposed; and in due course they will send in the bill to the Chancellor of the Exchequer . . .[1]

Attempts to introduce a measure of economy through Parliament have thus been usually doomed to failure. It would be untrue, however, to say that no effort to save money on the services is ever made by Parliament itself. Such an effort is made, in fact, repeatedly. It takes one of three forms. There is the attempt to save on fortifications, the attempt to save on uniform and the attempt to save on

[1] *Lord Randolph Churchill,* Rt. Hon. Winston Churchill. London, 1907, pp. 680-81.

military bands. For the selection of these three types of economizing there are profound psychological reasons. The British have rarely been enthusiastic about fortifications since about 1715, justification for their attitude deriving from their sad experience of such work. Either the fortifications have become obsolete before they could be attacked, and often indeed before completion, or else they are tamely surrendered as the sequel to fighting that has taken place elsewhere.

As for uniform and military music, there is a large body of British opinion that regards war as wicked and military ceremonial as more wicked still. To do away with the drums and colors would give more satisfaction to some than to do away with war itself. So the proposal to economize on all that is colorful and stirring will always awaken a glad response among those for whom the theatrical and the immoral are but different aspects of the same crime.

Overseas, recent economy on fortification has taken the extraordinary form of attempting to retain strategically the places to which we have given (or upon which we have forced) their political independence. A first discouraging experience of this policy in the Suez Canal Zone has not prevented us doing exactly the same thing in Cyprus, Singapore and (after some hesitation) in Malta. To bestow democratic freedom on a colony is a gesture which combines economy with virtue. It has the merit of being, sometimes, both popular and cheap; far cheaper, for example, than bestowing higher education or technical aid. Its sequel is apt to be an abrupt rise in local taxation. But while the garrison is substantially reduced, the theory lingers that the place is being held. The fallacy here is to suppose that it can be held after the water supply and the civilian labor have come under the control of what is now virtually a foreign country. And even were it otherwise, the troops still present, the apparently indispensable minimum, consist only of staff officers, orderlies, clerks, storemen, psychologists, technicians, canteen staff and occupational therapists. The theory is that the infantry can be flown back in case of need. While it is undoubtedly possible (if expensive) to fly troops out to Malaya or Cyprus, it is a fallacy to suppose that the same troops can then be flown to Gibraltar or Hong Kong. They are not available because they do not return for years and may not return at all.

Fortifications in Britain also afford scope for economy but of a different kind. They mostly date from 1845-60, many being designed to save England from Napoleon III. Some of these forts, built for coastal defense, have by now a certain nostalgic charm. They are slightly reminiscent of the cardboard citadels still to be obtained in toyshops. Some, though not all, of these centenarian structures had some slight relevance to the defense of Britain in 1940-41. With some misgivings, they were even occupied. They are still represented by blank spaces in the maps printed by a security-minded ordnance survey. It is now generally agreed, however, that their operational life is at an end. Battlements and drawbridges are thought to play no significant part in the warfare of the atomic age. So the moment would seem to have come for a quick sale at the best price that anyone will offer. The millions spent are gone for good. All that remains is the site value and an end to the cost of maintenance. But the land section of the War Department shows a great reluctance to part, finally, with anything; whether it be a beauty spot turned into a tank range or a citadel used for nothing at all. Its practice is to compromise, offering the site on a 99-year lease which is worth little or a 21-year lease, which is worth nothing. There are forts of great potential charm which are now being used as henhouses. Why? Does the War Department see a reversion to Victorian warfare a century hence? Even if it did, the fact remains that the forts might be requisitioned again in an emergency at any time. No, the War Department does not want the land nor does it foresee that it ever will. What it wants is the file, still open, for each property. For were the files closed, the question could be raised as to whether there might not be some economy in staff. When a freehold sale is actually made, the official preference is for a sale to another department or to a local government. In a recent instance of such a transaction the sum obtained was about a quarter of what had been offered by a private bidder. That the taxpayers' interests were involved was never, it would seem, the subject of a moment's consideration. Of financial responsibility there is seldom a trace. In its stead, we observe, more often, an inability to decide whether a place is wanted or not. Overseas, the compromise is to retain the base but withdraw the garrison. At home the compromise is usually to relinquish the fort but keep the file.

The attempt to save money on army clothing has for long taken the form of insisting that the uniform judged suitable for battle should also be worn on parade. This idea dates from the aftermath of World War I. While it certainly represents an attempt at economy, its result was a uniform not really suitable for anything; and realism in training was hampered by the soldier's knowledge that the uniform in which he was to crawl through a hedge today was to be speckless on church parade tomorrow. Behind this insistence on khaki was more, in fact, of puritanism than economy. Once it became apparent that the uniform for parade is not, and should never be, the uniform for battle, the question fairly arose as to why it should be drab in color. Why not blue or green or, for that matter, scarlet? But the idea that the uniform should appeal to romantic youth was even less acceptable than was the cost of supplying the extra cloth. So khaki it had to remain. Nor has the United States Army, as opposed to its Marine Corps, a better record in this respect. Even the new U.S. Air Force uniform is an unglamorous gray, while the Army has changed at vast expense and without manifest advantage from a drab brown to an equally drab green. It was the same urge toward petty economies in the wrong direction that abolished the British officer's cross-strap early in World War II (to save leather); this urgent reform being promptly followed by a decree that the officer's pistol should always be worn, a feat which without the cross-strap was all but impracticable. Attempts to economize in uniform seem to be uniformly unfortunate.

The same is true of the regimental band. Whenever there is talk of the need to economize, the abolition of the band is immediately urged. Few flourishing and obviously essential institutions have been abolished more repeatedly, and with as little interruption of their work. Here again, puritanism is at work. All that is colorful and stirring is the first target for economy, presumably because it ought to be among the last. And yet, what is the truth of the matter? If anything will attract the eagerness of youth, if anything will induce the likely youngster to enlist as a soldier, it will be the sound of the bagpipes or the squeal of the fife. The colors and the trumpets are the heart of the matter, without which there is little left. But this is so manifestly true that the decrees of abolition come automatically to nothing. Economies over fortification do actually take place and with a minimum of recovered expense. Economies over uniform have been made repeatedly and wrongly, and they at least have been carried out. But this folly over the band comes to nothing at the outset. To the rattle of the bureaucratic typewriter comes from afar the defiant bugle's reply and over distant hills the measured beat of the drums.

9

THE ANGLO-SAXON WASTE LINE

WASTEFUL WAR should give place, in theory, to the husbandry of peace. But the habit of waste is not, in practice, so easy to discard. People who grudge nothing in time of emergency seem often to have lost all sense of cost by the time the crisis has passed. They are prone to think that the effort made to save the country from alien conquest can be prolonged so as to save it from all the hygienic, economic and social ills from which it may be thought to suffer. No one paused during the war to question what the country could afford, for the one thing it could not afford was (obviously) defeat. So it was natural to ask why the same spirit of sacrifice should not be used to better purpose. Why not make war, but now on poverty and squalor?

When we consider this modern demand for expenditure in time of peace we find that it is largely concentrated on the types of expenditure which had been developed dur-

Osborn

ing the war. Wartime efforts have included the provision of hospitals, the paying of pensions, the education of orphans and the subsidization of food. It is partly due to the idealism and mental inertia of the many, partly due to the self-interest of the few that the peacetime expenditure and effort comes to follow the same grooves. The provision of hospitals ends in a national health service. The payment of pensions to veterans ends in the payment of pensions to everybody. Education of orphans ends in the education of all. As for food, the encouragement of the farmer and the subsidy of the grocer tends toward the uneconomical provision and distribution of whatever the last war had made us too often do without. All this might seem the natural aftermath of a state of siege. Nor is it possible to create wartime organizations for rationing and supply without also creating the vested interests of those to whom these departments have been entrusted. Quite apart from those interests, however, there is an undeniable appeal in the whole idea of using the national effort constructively, turning sword blades into industrial shares and building homes fit for heroes. Even the process of turning armies of soldiers into armies of officials will gain the approval of some, and other steps to combat unemployment may win the approval of all. About this postwar expenditure the only disconcerting and unwelcome feature is the final bill as presented to the nation. Incoherent as it may be in form, and as indeed it invariably is, its totals at least would seem to merit a scrutiny which they seldom receive.

Some very large amounts are spent these days on the acquisition and the dissemination of knowledge. Nothing could be more admirable in principle, few things as wasteful in practice. Whether in subsidizing research, providing education or publishing literature, governments seem unable to move without incurring the loss of millions. Everywhere there are intelligent people who will deplore the money spent on guided missiles and misguided colonies but who will insist that more, and still more, should be spent on universities and schools. There is a plausible case for this increased expenditure in that children multiply and knowledge expands. Against that, money can be wasted in good causes as well as bad, and evidence accumulates to show that such waste does occur.

Take research as an example. Research nowadays is so respectable a word that few have the courage to ask whether all expenditure under this heading is justified. On the one hand, the whole thing is wrapped in mystery. On the other hand, it is commonly assumed that research will pay an eventual dividend or at least that a failure to do research will have appalling consequences in terms of international influence and prestige. In all this there is an element of truth, but it is worth noticing that some large sums are involved. Great Britain, for example, had an estimated expenditure of £26,100,000 on Research and Development in 1958-59, with another £106,000,000 on Atomic Energy and separate research projects initiated and financed by the separate Ministries under the headings of defense, agriculture, medicine and so forth. Add to these figures a proportion of the vote for universities (£49,000,000) and the grand total reaches a very respectable sum. Is it conceivable that any part of this sum is wasted?

Waste is, of course, inseparable from research, inasmuch as negative results are necessarily frequent. But is the waste larger than is inevitable? There is good reason for thinking that it is but for reasons the opposite of what the layman might expect. The layman's suspicion is that money is lavished on dreamy-eyed eccentric professors who wander off vaguely and then reappear with demands for more, no one knowing what (if anything) they have discovered. They picture the scientist's approach to the civil servant in cinematic terms, the scientist being visualized as an oldish man with untidy white hair, a dirty woolen scarf and a wild gleam behind his spectacles.

"Glad to see you, Dr. Cloudesley," says the Assistant Under-Secretary. "I hope you have brought with you the papers we have been needing — the annual report for 1956 and the accounts of expenditure in 1955?"

"Well, no, actually. But I can tell you how things have been going. A year ago we thought we were on the brink of a great discovery, but we found this morning that the whole thing was based upon a small arithmetical mistake. You know — the decimal point in the wrong place . . . Poor Cartwright! Yes, yes, a sad business."

"You mean that Cartwright was disappointed at the failure?"

"Well, no. There was hardly time, was there? He *would* have been disappointed, of course, had he lived to realize the mistake we had made. A very sad loss. And the laboratory gone too!"

"The laboratory destroyed?"

"Oh, in an instant. All except that cupboard under the staircase where the janitor kept his brooms. That was saved by the fire brigade."

"Good God — that laboratory cost millions! And I expect Cartwright left a widow we shall have to pension?"

"Yes, indeed. Well, well, there it is. We shall have to

rebuild. Actually, we should have had to rebuild anyway. The laboratory was simply not big enough."

"All this is terrible news. But do tell me what you were trying to discover; in so far, I mean, as a layman can be expected to understand."

"Oh, didn't you know? Well, it *began* with a scheme to produce a new kind of fuel for use in rockets. Then we tried to see whether the same stuff would do as a preparation for removing old paint. We ended by trying to use it as a cure for coughs. Then it blew up. Very sad, very sad."

"And now you will be wanting a new grant to cover the next phase of your work?"

"That is really what I wanted to see you about. I can't give you any exact estimate, of course."

"No, no, I understand that."

"But it doesn't do to be niggardly. That only wastes money in the end."

"So you want, in effect, the largest possible grant?"

"Exactly! All you can get for us."

"Well, I'll do my best. Goodbye, and do please convey my sympathy to Cartwright's widow."

"Yes, yes, to all of them. Goodbye, my dear fellow. Better luck next time, eh? We do our best, you know. Can't do more. Goodbye, goodbye!" (exit, upsetting the dictaphone and taking the route which leads only to the central-heating plant).

That is the popular conception of how scientific work is supported by government; and it is completely false. Waste is the result of control being excessive, not of its being absent. But to understand the relationship between science and government we must go back to the beginning, to the reign of Charles II and the days of Sir Isaac Newton. It was Charles II who set up the precedent for later politicians and it would have been well if they had followed his example more closely. He set the pattern, first of all, by being personally interested in science and quite knowledgeable about its current progress. The Royal Society was royal in more than name, the King being in effect an active member and Prince Rupert more active still. There were problems, moreover, which Charles thought particularly important, notably the problem of ascertaining longitude at sea. But he made no effort to confine the scientists to that urgent problem and to that alone. Had his attitude been that of a modern politician, he would have talked to his leading scientist like this:

"Now, about this longitude affair. You know what the problem is, Dr. Newton. Our ships of war never know exactly where they are. They are always finding themselves off Hispaniola when they think they are entering New York."

"That would be an error, your Majesty, of latitude."

"Just so. Our seamen need to know their real position. And we all expect you men of science to help us. This is a matter of the utmost — of the utmost — I can't think of the word. What I mean is this, however: Solve this longitude problem and there would be no more confusing Finisterre and Ireland."

"And that would again be a mistake in latitude, your Majesty."

"Exactly. My captains have too much latitude and not enough longitude. We rely on you to put them right."

"I shall do my best, your Majesty. But there are other problems too. The other day I was in my garden . . ."

"Yes, yes, Dr. Newton. Very interesting indeed. Now

what I propose to do is to give you a government research grant. This will provide salaries for you and all these other Royal Society fellows. You can then all work on this longitude problem until you have solved it. No, no, don't thank me, I do this purely in the public interest. Allow me, nevertheless, to be the first to congratulate you on your new appointment."

"I am honored to receive your Majesty's commands. As I was saying, an apple fell on my head and it occurred to me . . ."

"Most unfortunate, most unfortunate. Luckily, we all wear hats, so that you have escaped with only minor injury and shock. Well, well, I must not detain . . ."

"But, this discovery of mine, your Majesty, which I have ventured to call the law of gravity . . ."

"*Thank you,* Dr. Newton — that was the very word I was trying to recall just now. This latitude problem is a matter, I was trying to say, of the utmost gravity. And now I must not detain you from your work."

(The audience is at an end and Isaac Newton withdraws. Enter Clifford, Arlington, Buckingham, Ashley and Lauderdale.)

"Come in, gentlemen. Forgive me for having kept you waiting. These scientists will *talk* so much. Now, about these Navy estimates . . ."

We need not follow the Cabinet Council proceedings further except to remark, in passing, that one item on the agenda is a request from Samuel Pepys for two assistants to help him cope with increased business at the Navy Office. The point, however, of this imaginary dialogue between Charles and Isaac Newton is that the modernized ruler does not know what he is talking about but is emphatic, nevertheless that one particular line of research is the one to pursue and the only one, therefore, to finance. The actual Charles II was, of course, a very different character. He knew a great deal about navigation. He had relatively little money for scientists, having spent most of it on girl friends who were no more grateful but far more decorative.[1] And he was just the sort of man to listen, fascinated, to the story about the apple. Mention of trees would, admittedly, have set him off once more on the narrative of how he escaped after the Battle of Worcester. But he would have grasped the point of Newton's Law (or Parkinson's Law, for that matter) long before his ministers had finished clearing their throats. Faced by Sir Isaac Newton, the modern politician would have known less, talked if anything more and ended by doing far worse than nothing.

The fallacy is to suppose that an elected Republican or Democrat can decide on a line of research and then leave the scientist to work out the details. No king or minister could have instructed Newton to discover the law of gravity, for they did not know and could not have known that there was any such law to discover. No treasury official told Fleming to discover penicillin. Nor was Rutherford instructed to split the atom by a certain date, for no politician of his day and scarcely any other scientist would have known what such an achievement might imply, or what purpose it would serve. Discoveries are not made like that. They are the result, as often as not, of someone wandering off his own line of research, attracted by some phenomenon hitherto unnoticed or suddenly seen in a new

[1] His Hanoverian successors were mostly to do the same but this is not regarded with the same disapproval or given the same publicity, either because they were Whigs or because their women were plainer.

light. Nowadays, when one country lags scientifically behind another equally prosperous country the most probable reason is that the government has been telling its scientists what they are to discover. This means, in other words, that too much money has been allocated to specific projects and too little to abstract science. The more resources have been devoted to projects the politician can understand, that is, to the development of discoveries already made and publicized, the fewer resources are available for discoveries which are now inconceivable in so much as they have not yet been made. The law which should govern scientific progress is that for every sum spent on a named project, a proportionate sum should be spent on science as such — that is, on University Science Faculties which are free to do as they like.

It may seem logical that the government which provides the money should decide how it is to be spent. But for it to insist on this right of control is very much as if the patient were to instruct his medical adviser, saying, "Since I am to pay the bill, it is for me to decide what the symptoms indicate and what the treatment should be." To this policy, one objection (of several) is that it means paying the doctor for nothing. His advice, if it is always to be what you want it to be, is worthless. If you are to tell him his business, you might just as well do without him altogether. In this context, doctors of science are in much the same position as doctors of medicine. Their advice is valueless if they are told by the layman what advice they are to give.

It is easy, in this context, to make a scapegoat of the politician, but the fact is that matters are made infinitely worse by public opinion and by the departments of government which are specifically concerned with it. The function of the Public Relation and Information Services, upon which vast sums are spent, is to present the public and the world with a favorable picture of what government is trying to do. This involves extracting from each department the information which may serve to illustrate this favorable view and which will provide matter for a press release. Upon organizations engaged in scientific and technical work the effect of these demands for information can be expensive and even fatal. Nevil Shute has told us, in *Slide Rule*, how the technicians employed on the airship R.101 were goaded into announcing progress and into fixing an early date for completion. The airship's construction had become not a technical experiment but a political issue. From a fairly early period in the story the final tragedy had become more or less inevitable.

The loss of life might have been partly justified if the right conclusions had been drawn from the disaster, but the same mistake has since been made repeatedly. Rockets are launched prematurely in deference to political pressure or public opinion. Radio and press releases drive scientists and technicians to death or catastrophe. Even when no lives are lost, the waste of money is fantastic. When the problem is one of dispatching a space ship to (say) the Moon, news of progress in Russia leads to frantic efforts in the United States; and the news of these efforts leads to fresh exertions in Russia. The absurdity and the tragedy is that a scientific or technical problem is being treated as a horse race. Where all depends on the thoroughness of experiment, preparation and trial, the actual result is imperiled by the introduction at the last moment of an irrelevant but apparently all-important question of prestige. Lives and effort have been repeatedly thrown away and final success postponed for years simply because of information services doing the work they are paid to do. So that to dispense with information departments would be not only an economy in itself, but an indirect economy in other ways. There is no need to tell the world or the public that a certain scientific venture is to be made. In many instances, there is no need even to say that it has failed. Keep the press release for the moment of success.

The contrary policy, as pursued today, might well be illustrated by an imaginary telephone conversation, as thus:

"Is that Dr. Thoroughgood? Smoothleigh here, of Information. Can you tell me, approximately, when your space ship (R.100 shall we call it?) will be completed?"

"Good heavens, no. There are all sorts of problems and difficulties."

"Do you mean that progress has been disappointing and that the project may have to be abandoned — or else given to some other team?"

"Certainly not. Our progress has been very satisfactory."

"When did the work begin then?"

"The decision to go ahead was taken by the Minister in April, 1950."

"And what was the estimate then of the time required for completion?"

"Very roughly, ten years."

"So that, with satisfactory progress, completion should be in 1960?"

"One can't be as precise as that. It was only a rough estimate."

"But to exceed it by (say) five years would surely mean that the progress has been disappointing?"

"Oh, I shouldn't say that. Besides, we won't take as long as that. Three years extra at the outside and possibly less."

"So we might *hope* for completion in 1962?"

"I suppose so."

"Very well then. May I issue a press release to that effect?"

"Not as a firm commitment."

"But as a reasonable expectation."

"Well, yes. If you think it essential."

"It will certainly be useful. It is public money that is being spent, you know. People like to know *how* it is being spent."

"All right. Say that we *hope* for completion in 1962."

"Early in the year?"

"How should I know? Say, by November."

In this way the technician is goaded into fixing a date. He thinks at the time that he has done no harm but he soon finds that his vague hope has become a fixture and has been printed in the calendar of forthcoming events. "Oh, well," he tells his colleagues, "it is useful to have a target date, whether we hit it or not." They do not believe him and he soon realizes that failure to announce completion on the expected date (now hardened to November 15) will discredit his whole team. At the end of 1961 he realizes the risks that are being run, but it is then too late.

"Now, about November 15," says the Information Officer. "I understand that the President is to be there for the launching. The reception afterwards has all been arranged but there is a problem about the massed bands. Will the music be audible above the rocket noises? Oh, and another thing: I have managed to get you a seat on the platform, at the end of the fifth row. That was difficult enough, and when it came to a seat for your wife — well, frankly, it couldn't be done. I did my best, but — there it is. I do hope she won't mind?"

"But, look, Smoothleigh, we never *guaranteed* completion by November 15. As likely as not, the space ship will be incomplete."

"Really, Thoroughgood, I hardly know whether to take you seriously. The whole thing is arranged now. Do you realize what a postponement will mean? What a blow to our prestige? And do you realize what it will mean if the Russians have their space ship launched before ours?"

"Do *you* realize what it will mean if the space ship rises a hundred feet in the air and then comes down on the platform?"

"Pessimist! Your team can do it if they really try. We *all* have the *utmost* confidence in you. And if you really have your doubts — well, a seat in the fifth row may have its attractions. Ha!"

"I shan't want the blasted seat. If everything depends on our success, there is only one place for me."

"What do you mean?"

"I shall be in the confounded ship itself. Good day and be damned to you."

This is, roughly, the process by which information services drive scientists and technicians to death and disaster.

While a great deal of money is being spent or misspent on science, very little goes to finance another type of research in which a smaller outlay might produce an even greater result. Where research is most obviously needed is in the technique of government itself. When the moment comes to launch the space ship, the equipment used will represent the latest thing in technical and scientific progress. The scientists in charge of the operation will be the leaders (we hope) in their respective fields of knowledge. All that is obsolete, by contrast, will be represented on the platform. There, under the awning and between the potted plants, will be grouped the politicians, the party chiefs, the religious spokesmen, the venerated community leaders and the accepted prophets of the age. And they will all be completely and utterly out of touch with the matter in hand. They will typify the government, the directing body and all that is most respected in our social system; the one part of our organization which we have completely forgotten to modernize.

Closely connected with the field of research, and linked with it by the universities, is the field of education. The frontiers of knowledge cannot be extended except by those who have absorbed the knowledge currently available; and the extension of knowledge then modifies the syllabus of those who come next to be taught. In considering the more wasteful aspects of education we must limit our inquiries to the classroom, to the expense of providing teachers, buildings, test tubes and chalk. In fact, as we know, people are largely taught what they are supposed to know about life by television, radio, cinema, newpapers and books; as also, and still more effectively, by each other. As a formative influence in society schools play a smaller part, in fact, than teachers are prone to imagine. As an item, however, of public expenditure, education comes high on the list; so high that its cost should be a matter of more than pensive interest to every taxpayer, and the more so in that much of the money is clearly wasted.

That this should be so is mainly due to the rise of an imaginary science of education, with a jargon of its own. This is known, technically, as educationalism. Broadly speaking, the difference between teaching and educationalism is that the teacher takes a difficult subject and strives to make it relatively easy, the educationalizer takes a simple subject (which he has failed to master) and makes it seem practically impossible. With the quality of education we are not here concerned, nor with the value of what is taught, but the chief result of educationalism is that everything takes very much longer and costs very much more. Education, like work, expands to fill the time available, so that years can be spent in educationalizing what used to be taught in as many weeks. Educationalism is also expensive in buildings and equipment. Schools have now to be built almost entirely of glass, so as to admit the sun, and have then to be fitted with plastic blinds in order to exclude it. Apart from that, however, a school filled with workshops and art rooms, buildings devoted to home economics and interior decoration, projection theaters and visual aids costs far more than schools consisting of ordinary classrooms and equipped with ordinary blackboards.

Studying the bill for all this apparatus, we come to realize that educationalism would be fantastically expensive even if it were of any value. As taxpayers we must pay not merely for the schools of every grade, but for the Teachers' College, for the Education Faculty and for numerous institutes of educational research. We have also to meet the closely allied costs of juvenile delinquency, as also the further expenses connected with the police, the reformatory and the prison. No one could say of educationalism that it is cheap. And the most expensive thing about it is the retaining in school of boys who will never benefit and who would be happier and less frustrated if allowed to earn their living. Juvenile misbehavior is largely the result of wasting the time of those who ought to be at work.

But the educational mission of government is not confined to the classroom. The adult citizen must also be pursued with exhortation, instruction and advice on any and every subject in which he might or might not show an interest. There are various ways of reaching the adult but one of the commonest is through the issue of publications. On these the waste of money has now reached gigantic proportions. It may seem inevitable that official printers should provide copies of legislation and verbatim accounts of what elected representatives are believed to have said in the course of debate. Whether the United States Congressional Record should include all that it does include is another matter. There would be something to be said for reprinting George Washington's farewell address twice each year if the Senators and Congressmen would only listen to it and especially to his warning against:

> . . . the accumulation of debt, not only by shunning occasions of expense, but by vigorous exertions in time of peace to discharge the debt which unavoidable wars may have occasioned, not ungenerously throwing upon posterity the burden which we ourselves ought to bear.

But the repetition of this message to a Congress which has balanced the federal budget only five times in the last twenty-seven years, incurring a debt of $283 billion, seems to produce no great result. Boondoggling, featherbedding and moonlighting continues, as also what Mr. Russell R. Smith rightly calls "the pouring of unconstitutionally collected taxes down foreign economic and political ratholes." But Washington would at least be worthy of attention if anyone would listen. The same would hardly be true of much that the Congressional Record contains; as for example the urgent news, breathlessly delivered, that the largest solid granite body in the world is Stone Mountain, located 16 miles east of Atlanta. It seems odd, again, that the House of Representatives should include in their record (Appendix) *An Exile's Rambles through Erin* by a resident of Peabody, Mass.; a poem entitled *The Revolt of the Muses,* written by one of the constituents of Mr. Hale Boggs; or even a *Tribute to American Indians* by the late Mr. Riley Thompson of Cloquet, Minn. There might be some conceivable point in thus recording *Lasting Foot-*

prints by Charles A. Shrewsbury, the Cowboy Poet of Buffalo, Mont., but what about the description of the International Pancake Day Race at Liberal, Kans.? Any congressman who moves that the House unanimously agree to place on record an *Ode to a Jellied Eel*, composed by one of his constituents, seems certain of gaining an absent-minded assent. It is only a question of time before someone puts in the New York Telephone Directory as an Extension of his Remarks. Its unanimous acceptance would be automatic.

But modern governments go far beyond printing records of debate, as we shall see, and one wonders at the outset why this should be so. It is the more easily understood, however, when we realize that many civil servants began their adult lives with dreams of authorship. They saw themselves, first of all, as dramatists, novelists, essayists and poets, only reluctantly accepting the role of bureaucrat. The more readily, therefore, do they plunge into print at the public expense. It is true that their works must often remain anonymous but they hope perhaps that the secret of authorship will leak out, giving them something of the dramatist's thrill who sees his name writ large on Broadway. "Look!" they fancy hearing the whisper, "there is the author of *Coccidiosis in Chickens!*" or "That man over there wrote *Expanded Nitrile Ebonite for Sandwich Construction.*" They imagine the awed "No — really? You don't say!" of those who thus learn these secrets for the first time.

To have written *Stem and Bulb Eelworms in Tulips* is not, to be sure, quite the same thing as having published a sonnet about daffodils. To have edited a work like *Di (Methyleyclohexyl) Phthalate and Methylcyclonexanyl Phthalate, Lead-Free*, satisfying as it may be as a feat of spelling, is not exactly like producing a new critical edition of Aris-

tophanes. Nor could the author of *Penetrant Methods of Flaw Detection* claim to rank high among the detective story writers. It is clear, nevertheless, that the civil servants have their quiet fun, as witness the title of one publication which reads *Teachers of Children Who Are Mentally Retarded*, a minor masterpiece of ambiguity. We must remember, moreover, that there are official best sellers. Who is likely to forget a book like *The Regression of the Node of the Quadrantids*, with its powerful plot, its strong human interest and stirring climax? Who can fail to recall the eerie supernatural overtones in *Techniques of manual preparation of spirit masters* (U.S. Government Printing Office, Catalog No. D.201. 6/7 : 804.1)? The official publication list is not without controversial works either. A book like *Training aid to assist dictators to perform better dictation* was bound to meet with democratic opposition, and a United States work on *First-class Post Offices* might easily occasion a nation-wide search to find them.

So the civil servants' temptation to write more and more official literature is at least understandable. What is disturbing is the mere quantity of the literature they do, in fact, produce. In the British volume aptly entitled *Government Publications 1957*, there appear, at first sight, to be 431 pages apart from the index. Closer study reveals the fact that the book begins at page 213, for no very obvious reason, being worse value (at 2s.) than might at first be supposed. When it is realized, however, that there may be anything up to fifty publications listed on a single page, the formidable nature of this list becomes apparent. Granting an average of twenty-three items to a page, there might be over 5000 publications in a single year. This output implies, we learn, a staff of 7000 and an annual paper consumption of 50,000 tons. Continents are being deforested, pulping machines worn out and papermakers kept working night and day to keep up with this appalling output of literature. An ordinary commercial publisher will print a spring and autumn list but it is reserved to H.M. Stationery Office to produce a *daily* list as well as a monthly catalogue. Of the £76,400,000 estimated British expenditure on "Common Services" in 1958-59, H.M. Stationery Office takes a very fair share.

We know, of course, that many official publications more than pay for themselves. When *The Alfalfa Weevil, How to control it* first appeared on the American bookstalls, there was an ugly rush of collectors eager to secure copies of the first edition. But it may be said of other publications that they are tedious and verbose, and of some that they are altogether needless. There is indeed a tendency to recapitulate the obvious even in the publication lists themselves, as witness the examples which follow:

> MAKING AND PRESERVING APPLE CIDER.
> Cidermaking is as old as the cultivation of apple trees. This bulletin presents information on the preparation and preservation of apple cider.
> (Catalog No. A1.9:2135) 10 cents
>
> GROWTH TRENDS IN MANUFACTURING INDUSTRIES: 1947-1956
> Presents the United States manufacturing growth trends for the period 1947-56. 20 cents

The first few words of these titles would seem to be self-explanatory but this is evidently considered a superficial view. So the title has to be explained. A pamphlet called *Growth Trends* does (paradoxically) deal with trends in growth. As for the first title and explanation, we are left in little doubt that a bulletin called *Making and Preserving*

Cider does in fact deal with making cider and preserving it. But this last example also serves to illustrate two other tendencies. For with repetition of the obvious is included the redundant and the doubtful. "Cidermaking is as old as the cultivation of apple trees." *So what?* When we are about to make cider, busy with piles of apples and receptacles of juice, how does it help us to have a civil servant putting his head through the window to remark that "cidermaking is as old as the cultivation of apple trees"? It is simply not relevant; and the further doubt arises as to whether it is even true. For what does the term "cider" mean? In the United States the word is used to describe unfermented apple juice. In England and France the custom lingers of describing the juice of the apple as apple juice, reserving the word "cider" or "cidre" for the same stuff when fermented. Cider, in this sense, can be powerful enough to cause havoc among the inexperienced, who tend to roll quietly into a ditch and stay there until sunset. To state that the making of real and alcoholic cider is as old as the cultivation of apple trees might well be true, although difficult to prove. Whether anyone ever drank "cider" in the American sense before 1900 might be even more difficult to establish. But these doubts arise only from a remark which is, in any case, totally beside the point.

Another class of publication common in the United States is the sequel to a Social Survey. Specialists in social surveying seem to congregate in greatest numbers in the United States Department of Agriculture. To judge from the literature produced by the Agricultural and Market Research Divisions, the Secretary for Agriculture must have an exciting life. At any moment a member of his research staff will burst into his office, panting for breath and full of the latest news. "Chief!" one will exclaim. "Do you know what? We have finished Report No. 13 of the *Household Consumption Survey* and here it is, 130 pages of it!"

"Swell!" says the Secretary, "and what does it prove?"

"Gosh, I can't wait to tell you. It's all about Home Baking, as you know. Well, just listen to this: 'At a given income, large households are more likely to bake than smaller households'!"

"Is that so? And what did the survey cost?"

"Only $122,000. But we have taken three years working on the results, which cost as much again. Add to that the printing and the paper. Cost is next to nothing."

"You sure did a fine job, son. Get me the White House! Wait till the President hears about this!"

He will scarcely have hung up when another executive hurries in with the *Market Research Report on Tobacco Smoking* (212 pages):

"What d'you know, Chief? We were *right* all the time! Age and income *do* affect smoking habits! We can prove it!"

"No!! You don't say?"

"We do say. Just look at these statistical results from regression analyses of the relation between cigarette consumption and income — you must allow, of course, for the standard error of regression coefficient."

"I'll do that. But what have you proved?"

"Why, that family demands on men of 25-54 are greater than in other age brackets!"

"You mean — ?"

"They smoke less."

"I got it! They have no money to buy cigars?"

"That's just it. They spent the money on diapers or toys or candy."

"Gee, you need *brains* to think of a thing like that. You boys have sure done a swell job. I'll not forget it. No, sir!"

Hardly will he have made this promise when two more statisticians fairly collide in the doorway. One of these, a middle-aged woman, gets going first.

"Mr. Secretary, here is the latest — *Teenage Girls Discuss Their Wardrobes* — 126 pages — and what a smart cover! Boy, is this good, or is it good?"

"Kid's stuff," says the other statistician, a youngish man. "Now look at this, Mr. Secretary — *Job Attitudes of Supermarket Employees*. Can you beat it?"

"Beat it yourself!" says the woman. "Now look, this is important. We have interviewed thousands of teenage girls. Just you guess what we asked them!"

"Well . . ." says the Secretary for Agriculture uncomfortably, "perhaps we had better not be too . . ."

"I'll tell you," interrupts the female statistician. "We asked them whether they bought their own clothes or whether they took their mothers along to the store."

"Gee, that's quite an idea! And what did they answer?"

"Some take their mothers. Some *don't*."

"Why, that's great!"

"But you haven't heard it all. No, sir! Sometimes they argue the matter and make a joint decision!"

"Is that so? I sure am glad to hear that. Very sensible of them. And now, son, what are you trying to tell me about Supermarkets?"

"Well, sir, we have been trying to find out what Supermarket employees think of their Store Manager."

"But how could you do that?"

"We asked them, sir."

"A very clever scheme. And what did they say?"

"Some liked him, some didn't, and some didn't know."

"Remarkable!"

"But there's more to come. We have discovered that sales per man-hour may be increased without increasing job dissatisfaction."

"It is good to hear it. And now, loyal colleagues, you must leave me to read these publications at leisure. The Department is proud of you!" For a Secretary of Agriculture life must be almost *too* exciting at times. Few men, one imagines, can stand it for long.

Most of these pamphlets about Home Baking or Cider-making or Anaplasmosis in cattle are for sale and may even be sold. But masses of publications are designed merely to give away. Among these some of the most fascinating are designed to persuade people to enlist or re-enlist in the armed services. To appreciate these as literature it is necessary to put them into historical perspective. In past centuries it was sometimes found necessary to print handbills for this particular purpose and the style of these will usually be found to reveal some psychological insight. The following example may be imaginary but is not untypical:

THE 8TH REGIMENT OF DRAGOONS
(The Duke of Wienerschnitzel's Own)

Commanded by that dashing officer, Lieutenant-Colonel the Lord Hellforleather, and soon to serve foreign under General the Marquess of Frothingrage, has still a few vacancies for smart young fellows of the right mettle. This crack Regiment is mounted on thoroughbreds and smartly uniformed in crimson and buff. It offers an active service to those with a taste for prize money. Rendezvous at the King's Head Inn, High Street, where all new recruits will be invited to drink His Majesty's Health.

N.B. Owing to the need to rest the horses, troopers will not be allowed to hunt more than twice a week.

(Signed) HUGH HACKWELL-SLASHEM
Captain and Adjutant.

GOD SAVE THE KING

We may suppose, if we will, that the 8th Dragoons had returned from an unsuccessful campaign with a quarter of its original strength. We may suspect, if we like, that Lord Hellforleather is aged seventy-three and that the regiment is to be sent, without him, to do garrison duty at Berwick-on-Tweed. We may conclude, finally, that the unit is indifferently mounted and that most of its horses are down with glanders. The fact remains, nevertheless, that the handbill has been cunningly worded. The recruit is offered drink and good fellowship, a smart and dashing uniform, a good horse, a glimpse of the world, a chance of some loot and almost certain death in some future cavalry charge. Why is this program attractive? Captain Hackwell-Slashem (whom we may picture as a seedy and shifty-looking person aged fifty-eight) knows exactly what he is doing. He knows, to begin with, that his potential recruit must be impelled by one or other (or perhaps a combination) of the following motives: he has been thrashed by his father, misunderstood by his family generally, jilted by his girl, sued for debt, or informed by another girl that her expected child is undoubtedly his. He wants first of all to drown his sorrows and then to make everyone repent having undervalued his worth. His former girl must briefly glimpse his gallant figure in crimson and buff, subsequently mourning his hero's death. His parents, receiving from him a substantial sum in prize money, will realize something of his noble character. And sundry creditors will appreciate (as will the expectant mother) that legal proceedings are unlikely to succeed. It is while vaguely daydreaming on these lines that a youngster (we will call him Tom) enlists, only to regret his decision next morning when the reveille sounds. Of such material as this a quite good soldier can be made.

Naval recruiting handbills also displayed, in past centuries, a deep psychological understanding of the type of youth they were meant to attract. Here again the author seems usually to have known what he was doing, as the following imaginary example may serve to suggest:

> H.M. SHIP ALLIGATOR
>
> That fast 32-gun frigate, commanded by Captain the Hon'ble C. U. Leighter, is ready to receive a very few prime seamen and smart landsmen. Large sums in prize money were paid out after the last cruise and she will shortly sail on detached service under the flag of Rear-Admiral Lyon-Waite. Join a service where the active are always noticed and where merit brings promotion. Rendezvous at the Benbow Inn, Portsmouth Point, where volunteers should inquire for Lieutenant Spinyarn.

Here again the thing explains itself and there is some faint possibility of the right men coming forward.

It is against this background that we must study the recruiting literature now printed for (say) the United States Government. It reveals an entirely different and contrasting attitude toward the career recommended. The emphasis is now not on romance or glory, not on the glamour of uniform or the pride of belonging to a daredevil unit, but on (of all things) security.

Some of the most interesting literature is not intended for issue to the potential recruit. At the end of his High School Education he is manifestly illiterate, as his certificate diploma practically admits. So the literature is intended for use by the man who interviews the recruit. It is expensively produced, nevertheless, and filled with snappy cartoons illustrating the happiness of army life and the misery endured by civilians. At this point it will be well to make the recruit an actual person. We shall call him Sid Trashcan, aged eighteen, and we may picture him as a dreary-looking gum-chewing dead-end specimen with longish hair, side-burns, and a drooping cigarette. He has been leader of a gang of social misfits at Whatsitville Tech; thinks himself tough but is actually quite unheroic, dreaming of all the brutalities he dare not commit. He is the logical outcome of modern educationalism. His subjects at school were consumer economics, world affairs, business technique, social studies, sex education, and problems in American democracy. That is to say, he knows nothing whatever. In a moment of hysterical self-pity he has decided to join the army and it is just possible that a year of being kicked around the parade ground would make something of him, if only in appearance.

Why should he want to join the army? His motives are exactly those of the eighteenth-century recruit who enlisted (see p. 176) in the 8th Dragoons. The circumstances, however, are modern and we shall suppose that Sid has *all* the motives of which Tom had only a selection. To be precise, he has been lectured mildly by the Whatsitville Tech Guidance Counselor, told by his mother that he is maladjusted, deserted by Susie (who is now going steady with Ed), informed at the drugstore that he can have no more Coca-Cola until he has paid for last week's, and finally told by Sadie that she is pregnant and that the fault is his. In point of fact Sadie runs no such risk and is suffering merely from indigestion, the result of too many bananas-split. But Sid believes her and thinks that the moment has come to leave for the war (if there is any) in Korea. The last straw, in this instance, is a harsh word spoken by the Guidance Counselor. After remonstrating with Sid about a recent incident — bottles thrown through the windows of the High School Beauty Parlor — the Guidance Counselor had concluded by saying "Gee, Sid, we should all like you to show more togetherness, more of the outgoing attitude. The way things are, we begin to think you self-centered and almost — well, I *must* say it — almost *unsocial.* We all want to help you get adjusted, Sid. We are all your friends, out to do our best for you. But, until we get this straightened out, there are folk around who will call you *Sissy.*" Sissy! That had been the deadly insult — to call Sid the Gangster "Sissy"! Sissy indeed! Sid would show them. Blind with tears, Sid has gone straight to the recruiting office, done with all this kid stuff and resolved, for the moment, on a heroic death.

He pictures the whole thing, and in technicolor too. The last men of the last company are huddled in the foxhole. Boom, Boom, go the bursting mortar bombs, Rat-tat-tat-tat-tat go the machine guns. "Wait here, you guys," says Sid, "I'm gonna give the K.O. to that darned bunch over there. Mortar bombs, heck — they can't do this to me!" The others all try to hold him back. "No, Sid, you'll jest get killed for nothin," says the Master Sergeant (Burt Lancaster). "We can't do without you, Sid," pleads the Lieutenant (Kirk Douglas). "No, No, No!!" screams the hospital nurse (Brigitte Bardot). "I come with you — yes?" But Sid has time for only one kiss — lasting ten minutes — before he must break from her, saying "No, kid — this is something bigger than either of us." He adjusts his helmet and fingers his tommy-gun. "Hold that girl, Sarge. S'long, you guys. This is it!" He dashes from the trench, firing the first five hundred rounds from the hip. Five hundred of the enemy are killed but there are thousands more. He charges on, throwing his first grenade. The enemy battery is silenced, but their tanks are (oddly enough) unharmed. He fires another thousand rounds, each one finding its target, and now he is right on top of the enemy mortar and its crew of twelve. He shoots five, kicks four unconscious and strangles two with his bare hands. The twelfth treacherously stabs him in the back with a penknife. Sensing that the climax is meant to be tragic, the nurse breaks from the Sergeant and runs toward where Sid lies dying. Rat-tat-tat-tat goes a machine gun from one of the enemy tanks, firing quite illegally on the Red Cross. The bullets, aimed to a nicety, rip off her battle dress and allow her to fall, half naked, into the dying hero's arms. A shell bursts, buries them both, and we glimpse the two crosses which afterwards mark the spot. The scene changes abruptly to the Trashcan home, where the General (Fredric March) has been breaking the news to Sid's parents. He comes slowly down the garden path and pauses at the gate. On the opposite sidewalk the Whatsitville High School Guidance Counselor is sitting with his head in his hands. But the General is staring beyond him into the sunset as he utters the closing lines, "Where do we get such men?" (*pause*) "Where do we get them?" (*fade-out*).

This is the scene which is being enacted in Sid's fevered imagination as he enters the recruiting office. A smiling Guidance Counselor (in uniform) adjusts his bifocal spectacles and invites Sid to make himself at home. He offers him a glass of Pepsi-Cola and another cushion. "So you are thinking of joining the army, Mr. Trashcan?" says the Sergeant-Counselor. "And a swell idea, too. Before we go on, may I call you Sid? That's just swell." Fingering his publicity sales aids, the Sergeant goes on with the smoothness of long experience. "And why is it a swell idea, you ask? I'll tell you. It's because you are well paid, regular as clockwork. But, that is only a part of what you get. The army offers you FREE, food and clothing, lodging and medical care, retirement equity and legal counsel. It offers you SECURITY! Now, what branch of the service did you think of joining?"

"The infantry!" says Sid, still dying heroically among the shellbursts. The Sergeant looks almost shocked.

"Whatever gave you that idea?" he asks. "Now, look, son. I'm going to give you some good advice. It's far better to choose something technical. We don't really need infantry these days. Aim at some service with specialty training and extra pay."

"O.K., then," says Sid, looking Death in the eyes. "What about parachute service?"

"See here, Sid," pleads the Sergeant, "be your age. Why go parachuting when you can have a nice steady job as teleprinter, driver or cook? Some day you will have dependents to consider!"

"Dependents?" says Sid with a groan.

"Yes, dependents. Supposing you marry some nice girl. Let's call her Sadie."

"SADIE?"

"Yes, Sadie. Well, the time would come when you had a child. Twins, maybe."

"TWINS??"

"Or even triplets. That is when you have to think of the

future. Now the army helps you to build a house of your very own. Lends you up to $17,000 with only 5 per cent down and twenty-five years over which to pay it back. More than that, the army gives you a comfortable retirement income. It is far more than a pension because you still get army privileges when you retire. You can use the thrift shop and the army gasoline station. You can use — I mean Sadie can use — the army beauty parlor. In the army you are secure for life: but you want to choose the right branch. Now I'll give you a hint. I wouldn't do this for everybody but I kinda taken a fancy to you, bud. And what I say — this is strictly between ourselves, mind you — what I say is 'Go to the Army Information School; or else to the Finance Corps.' When it comes to real security for the future, civilian life has nothing so good to offer."

"But I thought of going overseas."

"And so you can — so you shall. The place to go is Hawaii. Boy, will you have a good time in Hawaii! The very place to continue your higher education, with correspondence courses and group study as well. A regular world tour you can have at the same time, with bathing beaches, swimming pools and Coca-Cola brought right to your easy chair in the shade."

"Gee, I'm not that old."

"Ah, but when you are, think what it will be like to own your own ranch house, your own car and television set. There you will sit with Sadie beside you . . ."

"Sadie!!"

"Well, I just chose that name for an example. It might be Susie. As I was saying, then: there you will lie in your hammock, with Susie reading a kid's book to her grandchild . . . Hell, what's the matter? Where has the feller gone?"

Sid has taken to his heels, sobbing with frustration, and anyone might conclude that the army is none the worse for losing this unpromising recruit. That is true but the township of Whatsitville is much the worse for having to keep him. And this local disaster is largely due to issuing the Sergeant with the wrong literature, expensively printed on glossy paper with witty illustrations in three colors, all clipped together with a plastic spring. The fact is, the Sergeant would have done better if left to himself.

The fallacy in all the literature is by now apparent. Young people in search of security (they are surprisingly numerous) are unlikely to join the armed forces at all. They can be more obviously secure in other ways. Supposing, however, that the advertising technique were entirely successful, what sort of army would there be? The resulting army would be a collection of uniformed civilians — barbers and clerks, medical orderlies and chiropodists, telephonists and cooks. When the bugle sounds the charge, there is not a bayonet to be found. Should a modern Custer seek to make a last stand he has to rally the personnel of the information branch, hoping against hope for the clatter of typewriters to the rescue. This is not magnificent and it is not war; and the future disasters for which we are providing can be largely attributed to this flood of paper which pours forth from official printers and threatens to swamp the deforested earth.

One might imagine that a shortage of paper would tend to check this flow of governmental literature. But the experience of Britain in World War II goes to prove that it is everyone else who has to go without, the official printer redoubling his efforts out of mere patriotism. A collection of British government circulars issued in 1939-45 would be more impressive in bulk than in content. Many would be found to be instructions as to how the citizens should use impracticable means to counter imaginary dangers. And literature issued before the war, but in preparation for it, would be found to have been then (as now) a waste of paper, impeding rather than helping what was in any case a misdirected effort. Under stress of paper shortage, government departments can be induced to use the same envelope on repeated occasions but no shortage so far experienced has ever induced them to restrict their flow of exhortation, warning and advice.

There are some who would observe, at this point, that the cost of printing and the cost of paper represent only a fraction of administrative expense considered as a whole; and this may well be so. But a true estimate of cost must include the civil servant's time. A little investigation would show that this official verbiage is more expensive than would at first appear, wasting the time of author and recipient alike. It takes time, remember, even to open the envelope, identify the contents and throw it in the wastepaper basket. It has taken far longer than that to write and it is fair to ask whether the author (and his team of assistants) if denied the opportunity of authorship, would be wanted at all. Anyway, the experiment might well be tried of ordering each government department to publish next year just half the number of words it issued the year before. If the results were as satisfactory as seems probable, the same order might be repeated the year after that, and so in successive years until the present roaring torrent had become a babbling brook, and the brook in turn become the merest trickle, and the trickle becomes no more than the dripping of a faulty tap . . . drip . . . drip . . . drip . . .

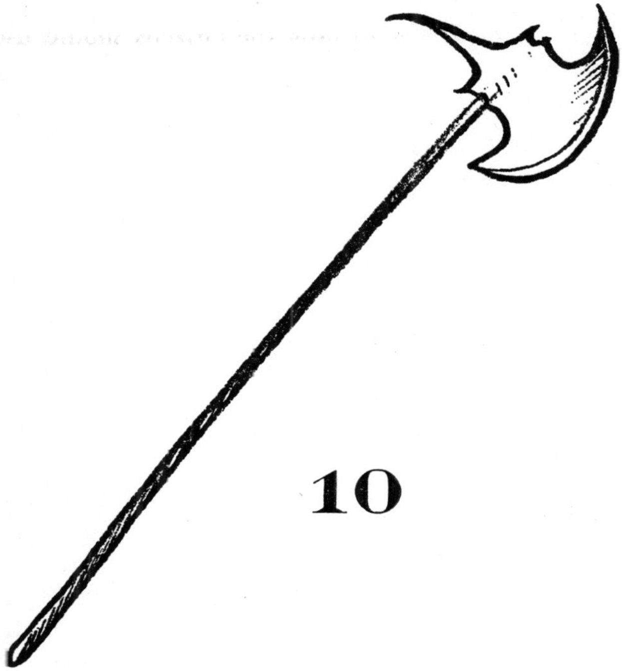

10

ABOMINABLE NO-MEN

It is often supposed that government departments have their own internal checks on expenditure, their own financial experts and, for that matter, their own inertia, itself a check on new extravagance. It is now known, however, among students of Wastage, that internal efforts to achieve economy are invariably the prelude to additional expense. This is more especially true of attempted economies in defense (as we have seen in Chapter 8) but it is also generally true in all departments of state. To begin with, the internal auditors have their own tendency to multiply. The economic advisers (like the departmental groups of lawyers, physicians and architects) are an expense in themselves. And what do they achieve? They make a careful check on the use of postage stamps and stationery. They query items of travel expense. They pursue the individual who has been inadvertently overpaid. But in all this petty activity they fail to recover the total of their own salaries. They save us nothing.

To say that they save us nothing is in fact an understatement. What they actually do is to ensure that no saving occurs. For each subdepartmental chief knows that a failure to expend his annual allocation will lead to a permanent reduction of the sum to which he is entitled. He knows, further, that what he thus saves will be reallocated to the subdepartment which has overspent, the head of which will then be promoted in recognition of his widening responsibilities. So he must plan for a small deficit each year, knowing that to do otherwise would be unfair to his subordinates if not to himself. This principle runs all through the public service down to the headmaster of the primary school, struggling to spend his generous allowance for "extra" equipment; and down indeed to the soldier in the overheated barrack room heaping coke on the stove so as to ensure that next week's supply may be obtainable. This sort of internal watchfulness leads only to eternal waste.

The Treasury is, as we have seen, the official safeguard

against extravagance but its failure in this role is manifest. Officials of the Treasury are vigilant enough but they work within narrow limits. Let us take, for example, an imaginary department, the British Ministry of Inter-Departmental Co-Ordination, created by the late Mr. Ramsay Macdonald as a necessary feature of the Welfare State but since amalgamated with the Ministry of Abortive Planning. It is headed by the Secretary of State for Co-Ordination and Planning and its staff has recently moved to new offices next to Scotland Yard but with detached accommodation elsewhere; notably in Bush House, at Maida Vale, Kensal Rise, Hackney Wick and Penge. Its 7000 employees at Buff Orpington are soon to be moved into larger premises at Cheltenham and Bath. Treasury officials descend periodically on this ministry and express horror, as well they may, at the steep rise in its estimates. The Chief Planner has to fight for every thousand square feet of office space. The Permanent Under-Secretary for Co-Ordination has to make out his case for every stenographer. But it is not the Treasury's task to enquire whether the Ministry ought even to *exist*, which is clearly the first question to ask, and one to which a reply in the negative would save further and detailed scrutiny of its expenditure. In Treasury practice a precedent for expenditure is the great thing. Once a department has its Vote, no one at the Treasury is likely to query its claim to survive. It spends and therefore is.

Considering such a state of affairs, the reader may find it difficult to understand how this growth can have come about. He will at some time have had the experience of approaching a department of government with an application, a suggestion, an inquiry or complaint. He will have discovered, at some stage of this encounter with bureaucracy, an obstructiveness beyond all previous example. Remembering this, he will wonder perhaps how government departments should have become so large and costly. For the obstructiveness remarked by the supplicant taxpayer should by rights have impeded the department's growth. The officials so ready to say "No" to him ought to have been as eager to say "No" to each other. An automatic resistance to any and every proposal should be a check in itself on innovation and therefore on expense. That there is logic in this argument is not to be denied, but the reader will realize, after further meditation, that his premises are false. The problem is not as simple as he has been tempted to suppose. Not all civil servants, to begin with, are obstructive. Some of them are very much the reverse. We must also remember that resistance to every suggestion includes resistance to every suggested means of reducing expense. In the pages which follow, therefore, an attempt will be made to describe what actually happens to the average applicant, relating this experience afterwards to the process by which administration expands. After wading through a great deal of irrelevant material, thrown in to impress him with the author's knowledge, the reader will come to see that his own experience of administration (as seen from the outside) is not inconsistent with the statistics of departmental expansion.

In attempting to elucidate this problem, we must not ignore the work done by previous scholars. In paying this tribute to our predecessors in a given field of research, the technique is to describe them as learned, meticulous and brilliant and then go on to demonstrate, in all but words, that we ourselves are better in all respects. This method was first discovered in World War I by the officer who recommended his orderly for the Victoria Cross, explaining simply that "he never left my side throughout the action." It is strictly for this purpose that we now refer to the epoch-making discoveries of Professor P. G. Wodehouse, frankly admitting at the outset that many of our basic concepts in public and business administration derive from him. These are now so much a part of contemporary thought that their origin is often forgotten. No one can now recall a time when Yes-men and Nodders were not sharply differentiated in the textbooks but seldom is credit for this useful distinction given to the scholar who first perceived wherein the difference lies. Among the few, however, who remember Wodehouse's first brilliant paper (read before the Royal Society in 1929) there is a feeling of regret that his attention was never drawn to the opposite subspecies; the No-men and the Shakers. The paradox here (and it is time we had a paradox) is that the layman, the downtrodden taxpayer who reads this book, is aware only of the No-men while the first scholar to classify the object now under the microscope saw only the Yes-men and the Nodders. It may seem presumptuous to draw distinctions where as great a scientist as Wodehouse could perceive none, but some further classification would be at least convenient even if we recognize that it cannot be final.

Having thus established the relationship between the present author and the scholar hitherto regarded as preeminent in this field of research, we go on to deal brusquely with a rival of about our own seniority. We do not mention him by name for this would be to give his work a significance which it scarcely merits. Our references to a rival must be decidedly oblique, as the sentences which follow may serve to illustrate. The attempt has been made (we begin casually) to show that administrative organizations, whether governmental or industrial, have two vertical divisions. There is on the one hand the division through which decisions taken on the highest level are filtered down to the pyramid's base. There is, on the other hand, the division through which applications, suggestions and appeals make their way from the base to the summit. These two divisions seldom correspond to those which exist on paper but the theory has been put forward that the chain of communication on the executive side goes from the Chief to the Knowman and so to the Yes-men (Senior and Junior) and at last to the Nodders. According to the same initially plausible argument, the incoming proposal is dealt with on the contemplative side by the Shakers, the No-men (Senior and Junior), the Don't-Knowman, and eventually the Chief. There are, however, two major objections to this theory (which we mention only to demolish). In the first place, it does not tally with our experience, nor with the reader's. In the second place, it does not explain how any idea ever reaches the Chief at all. It is now widely recognized among those whose opinion carries weight that the contemplative side of an organization is seldom if ever entirely negative. What we actually find is that the two types *alternate* at different levels. We thus observe the Admirable Willingman alternating with the Abominable No-man. We perceive, as others apparently cannot, that Nodders intermingle with the Shakers. To the man from outside the hierarchy with an idea to sell, the effect is one of alternating despair and hope; an effect best to be described in narrative form:

Picture, to begin with, the Head Office or Ministry,

with the apprehensive visitor on the threshold. Beneath his left arm is the Scheme, the Plan, the Brainwave or Blueprint. Trembling slightly, he is shown into the office of Mr. Jolly D. Goodfellow, who wears country tweeds and an Old Receptonian tie.

"Come in, Mr. Hopefall. Take the armchair. Do you smoke? Forgive me a moment while I send for your file. Valerie, would you mind bringing the file on the Hopefall Project? I had it yesterday . . . Ah, here it is! Thank you, Monica: you look very glamorous today — a lunch engagement? All right, we shan't expect you back until three-ish . . . Now, here is the file, right up to date. I have studied your scheme very carefully and can see no objection to it. In fact, I think it most ingenious. We should all congratulate you on the method by which you propose to overcome the main technical difficulty. A neat solution, lucidly explained. The scheme has my fullest support."

"We can go ahead, then?" asks Mr. Hopefall, scarcely able to believe his ears.

"Yes, yes, certainly!"

"What — now?"

"Yes, immediately. Well, *almost* immediately. As soon as we have the Chief's signature. I foresee no difficulty of any kind."

"You can't approve it yourself?"

"Well, no, not exactly. But I can advise the Deputy Assistant. *He* can approve it straightaway; and I expect he will."

"That is terribly kind of you."

"Not in the least. We are here to serve the public, I always say; not to create difficulties just for the love of obstruction. We are definitely out to help all we can. That is our job . . . Now, I have added my strong recommendation on the minute sheet. All I need do now is to sign it — so. And we might do well to accelerate the process a bit. Valerie, do be a dear and find me an URGENT label in red. Thank you, that's fine. See that this file goes *direct* to the Deputy Assistant. Come back tomorrow at this time, Mr. Hopefall, and you should be able to go ahead on the following day. Ask for me personally and telephone Extension 374 if you have the least difficulty. It has been a pleasure meeting you, Mr. Hopefall. Goodbye for the present, and all good luck with your project. You have nothing further to worry about."

On the next day, Hopefall is told that the Deputy Assistant can see him at 12.30. After waiting in the outer office, he is shown at 1.45 into the small bare room occupied by Mr. Ivor Snagge, who wears deep mourning, rimless spectacles and a shifty expression.

"Ah, Mr. Hopefall, I have been studying this scheme of yours . . ."

"I trust my memorandum sets it out adequately. If there is anything I can explain more clearly, I shall be glad to do so."

"That won't be necessary. The proposal is clearly described. The trouble is . . . (Miss Tightlace — shut this window, please. There's a draft!) . . . What was I saying? Ah, yes. The trouble is that the scheme is impracticable, unacceptable and quite possibly illegal. It is, to my mind, *completely* out of the question."

"Oh, but *why?*"

"Completely and utterly impossible. I should have thought that even Goodfellow would have realized that. On financial grounds alone."

"But, surely — "

"Out of the question, Mr. Horsfall. The objections to the plan are as numerous as they are insuperable. (Miss Tightlace — wedge some paper under that window — I can *still* feel a draft.) No, Mr. Horsfall, it cannot be done."

"Are you sure that you have the right file before you? My name is not Horsfall but Hopefall."

"So you think I would deal with a matter of this kind without studying the right file?"

"Well, you hadn't the right name."

"And that proves that our whole procedure is careless, haphazard and lax?"

"I never said that."

"I think you did."

"In that case you are prejudiced against me and should refer the matter to higher authority."

"That is what I intend to do. Nor do I doubt for a moment that the file will then go to the Public Prosecutor. In the meanwhile, I must ask you to leave this office before I send for the police. No violence, please! Your application is rejected. That is final, and you will gain nothing by abusive language. Good day to you, sir."

Ten days later Mr. Hopefall will be edging nervously into the presence of the Assistant Director, wondering what to expect this time. He need not have worried, however, for Mr. O. H. Gladleigh is both helpful and charming.

"I have a minute here from Snagge but we won't take that too seriously. I expect you saw him about lunch time. A most conscientious worker, you know, but a bit testy after midday. Now, about your proposed scheme, I can see no real objection to it. In principle it should be accepted. I only wish I could do that at once on my own authority. In view, however, of the points raised by Snagge, I think it will have to go to the Deputy Director. I shall strongly advise him to authorize the scheme, treating the matter as one of high priority."

A week later Mr. Hopefall will march confidently into the Deputy Director's office, to be confronted by a tall, thin man of haggard appearance staring hopelessly into some dreadful futurity. This is Mr. Longstop. He holds the file limply and motions his visitor to a chair. There is a silence of a minute or two, and then Mr. Longstop sighs, "No." After another minute he mutters, "Can't be done . . ." Then at last he asks:

"Have you considered all the difficulties? Financial? Political? Economic? Have you assessed the probable reaction overseas? Have you tried to judge what the effect will be on the United Nations? I am sorry, Mr. Hopefall, but I have no alternative. What you propose is, frankly, impossible."

He will end by referring the matter again to higher authority. Nor need we follow the file to its logical conclusion. It is already apparent that the Admirable Willingmen alternate in sequence with the Abominable No-men. The final decision must depend, therefore, upon the number of levels in the organization or (to be more exact) upon the relative position of the level at which the decision will be made.

From a study of this administrative behavior pattern it is possible to lay down certain principles to be observed by those who approach the organization. The first rule, clearly, is to persist. The applicant who left the building forever after an interview with Snagge or Longstop would never have met Mr. Gladleigh nor spoken with Longstop's superior, Mr. O. K. Oldmann. The best policy, it must be obvious, is to persevere until you find a Willingman. The situation is that familiar to us all when we are shopping. The assistant says at once "No, we have no Sopvite Shaving Cream. There is very little demand for it." The experienced customer perceives at once that the assistant is too lazy to see whether he has the stuff or not. He decides, therefore, to wait. He finds a stool and settles down with an air of limitless patience. In ten minutes the assistant, sick of the sight of him, produces the Sopvite, muttering that he has found an odd tube left over. He will in fact have opened a new crate but there is no need to comment upon this. The point is that persistence has won. In the imaginary examples quoted the various executives have automatically referred the proposal each time to higher authority. In real life they might not have done this. The technique, therefore, is to sit patiently until they do. It is needless to say anything much. Just sit and stare at the executive until exasperation forces his hand. Inclination and habit will alike induce him to refer the matter to someone else. You will then have scored a point, for the other man can hardly be more obstructive and may well be less.

The second rule is to make use of the Willingman when you have found him. Your object this time is to obtain a decision and prevent reference to the next higher level. You will know from experience that a Willingman's superior is normally a No-man. You must, therefore, convince the Willingman that the decision can be his. The technique should be one of regret that so trifling a matter should have been allowed to reach so senior an executive.

"I am really ashamed," you will repeat, "that your time should be occupied in this way. It is satisfactory for me, I will admit, to discuss the question with a man actually responsible for making big decisions. One tires of underlings. But this problem scarcely deserves your notice."

Expanding in the warmth of your admiration, the Willingman may sign his approval there and then, irrevocably committing his superiors to a policy of which they know nothing; and this is exactly what you want.

The third rule is to avoid wasting time on the No-man once he has been identified. It is a common error to suppose that the No-man could be convinced by argument and might eventually say "Yes." But that is to misunderstand the No-man's character. His automatic negative does not arise from any rational opposition to your scheme as such. He says "No" because he has found that this is the easiest way and because he never says anything else. Should he say "Yes" he might be asked to explain the reason for his enthusiasm. Should he approve, he might be involved in work resulting from the proposal's acceptance. Should the scheme prove a failure he might be held responsible for advocating it in the first place. But saying "No" is relatively safe. It requires no explanation because those higher in the organization need never know that the proposal was ever received. It involves no work because no action follows. Nor can the scheme fail for it will not even be tried. The only danger is that the applicant may gain a hearing some other way; but even later acceptance of the plan need not worry the No-man unduly. He cannot be held responsible for any failure and will not be asked to aid in ensuring success. Few will remember his opposition and those who do can be told that the plan *in its original form* was impracticable and that its effective application owed much to the process of healthy criticism to which it was subjected in the early stages of its development. The No-man has little to lose.

The successful application of the principles here revealed depends not upon argument as to the merits of the case but upon a preliminary survey of the organization. The correct procedure is to count the number of levels and discover where the No-men are placed. Make a chart of the whole structure indicating the No-men as so many black squares in the crossword puzzle. Then plan your campaign so as to avoid the black squares, sidestepping from one Willingman to the next, and so reaching the lowest level at which a decision is possible. In an organization of executives who always say "Yes," and executives who always say "No," the problem is not one of argument but of pattern. The navigator does not argue with rocks; he avoids them. That this is the right policy is apparent to anyone who knows that the rocks (the No-men) exist. As against that, it would be wrong to imagine that these elementary principles comprise the whole of knowledge. The problem of nomanity, as here defined or at least described, awaits detailed investigation. Our researches have scarcely begun.

It would be premature even to suggest the outline of a research program, but there is one experiment which could perhaps form a useful point of departure. This would begin by the assembling in one place of all the No-men from a given and typical area. The object of the conference, as announced, would be to report on the nature and philosophy of Nomanism. The most negative of the No-men would be elected to the Chair and the program would include a series of discussions on the sort of topics which No-men might appreciate. These should include:

1. *Opening Session.* Major objections to the conference being held.
2. *Lecture.* Objections to the program as proposed and reasons why no other program can be drawn up.
3. *Debate.* The impossibility of continuing work in public session.
4. *Debate.* The impracticability of forming committees.
5. *Informal Discussion.* The principal drawbacks inherent in all the excursions so far planned to places in the vicinity conspicuously lacking in interest.
6. *Lecture.* Some reasons for doubting whether the closure of the conference is even feasible.

No single one of these discussions would actually take place. For one thing, the objections to each subject would probably prove insuperable. Apart from that, however, the first session would also be the last. For the essence of the scheme would be to hold the Congress of Comparative Nomanism on a raft in the middle of a large deep-water lake. As soon as the delegates had all arrived and as soon as the opening session had fairly begun, those responsible for the experiment would quietly open the sea-cocks and head for shore in the only available boat. As the murmurs of negation died away, and as the last portion of the raft sank out of sight, those in the boat would turn to each other with a smile. They would share for an instant the scientists' satisfaction in a first experiment's complete success. Then, as night fell on the quiet lake, the rhythm of the oars would begin afresh and the boat would glide on toward where lights appeared on the darkening shore.

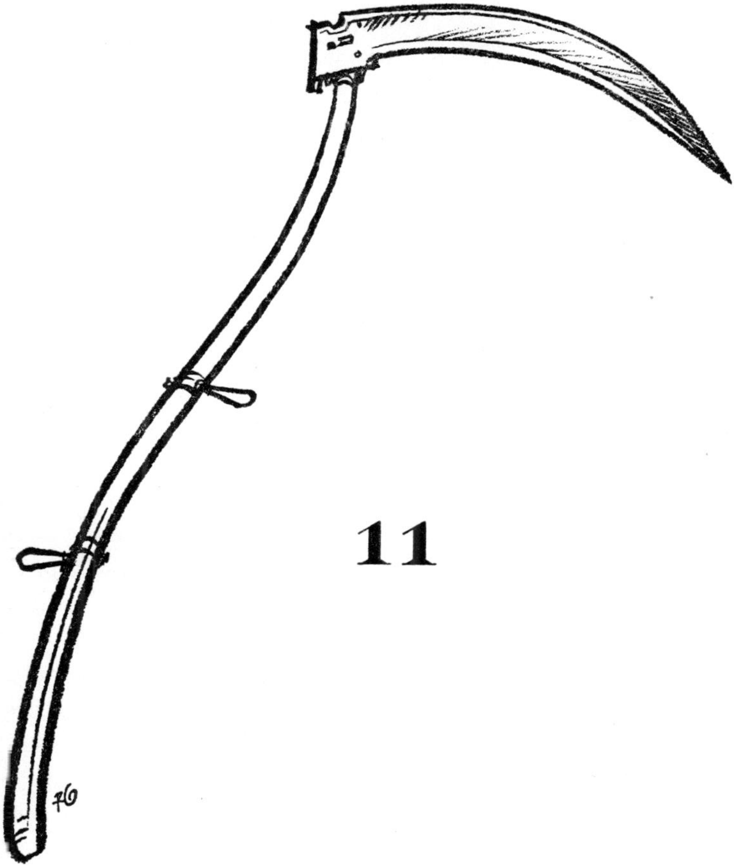

11

THE AMERICAN BUST

Compared with Britain, America is a vast area with enormous resources and a huge revenue. Its waste is proportionately gigantic, as befits a country with a $62.4 billion budget, a federation employing 2.3 million civil servants and listing them on a $9 billion payroll. But if American waste dwarfs even the waste observable in Britain, it must be realized that the United States (unlike the British Isles) has the capacity still for reform. The country which elected President Harding also elected President Hoover, and it is to him (when out of office) that the United States owes the magnificent series of the Hoover Commission Reports. Had Britain ever produced anything comparable, the whole thing would have been shelved and forgotten like Lord Rothermere's Anti-Waste League of 1921, but Herbert Hoover can claim that "Economies totaling $7 billion can be traced to the first Commission's report. And we are on our way to savings of upwards of $3 billion a

year as a result of the second Commission's recommendations." With respectively 72 and 64 per cent of their recommendations accepted, the members of these two Commissions have performed a miracle both of finance and political education. Their example should give new hope to the world.

But while the Hoover Commissions have had such startling success, the fact remains that the wastage was there for them to investigate and that a good percentage remains for them to deplore. The greatest achievements of the Hoover Commissions are Public Law 599 (for defense unification) and Public Law 759 (for modernized federal budgeting), both passed and signed by the President in August, 1958. There can be little doubt that one result of modernized budgeting, will be to reveal still further wastage. When it is realized that the federal government spends $700 million annually on collecting information and $100 million each year on issuing directives; when it is grasped that civil servants produce a yearly crop of 127,000 reports and that the Employers Quarterly Federal Tax Return Forms require 184 million lines of information from employers, not merely once in a while but every single year, the extent of wasted effort begins to become apparent. When so much is understood, it only remains to grasp that the same scale of waste is repeated all over again at the successive levels of state, county, city and district. With an undoubted capacity for reform, the United States has also an abundance of raw material.

A study of waste in the United States must begin with the question of foreign aid. It was pointed out in 1952 that Mr. W. Averell Harriman had been given $7,328,903,976 to scatter in largesse about the world, plus another unexpended billion from the previous year. By 1955 the United States postwar spending on foreign aid had reached the not inconsiderable total of $50 billion, the money being then distributed by some thirty-four distinct and unrelated agencies. A total of 115,250 people (30,681 of them being American) have been employed overseas on work connected with this program. The Hoover Commission studied this situation, noted a vast and uncoordinated expenditure but concluded that economic assistance should continue in order "to secure the maximum military security for ourselves and to take our part in the advance of the living standards of the free world." The Commission was given to understand that the nonmilitary aid program would help also to defeat communism. A study of the situation, however, left members of the Commission wondering whether this was really the effect of what was being done. After an expression of skepticism on this point, they went on to suggest that the various streams of benevolence (if they are to continue) might at least be related to each other in some other way. With that cautious conclusion no sane person is likely to disagree.

Where the doubt arises, among a few critics of American policy, is whether this economic aid serves any useful purpose of any kind. It is a question of whether the whole plan is not based on false psychology. The basic assumptions are that people who have been given economic aid will be more prosperous and less likely therefore to turn communist, and that their gratitude will incline them toward friendship with the United States. Many Americans have a rather pathetic desire to be liked and it finds expression in such a policy as this. They assume further that gratitude and friendship can be retained by reminding the peoples concerned of their indebtedness to American aid. For this purpose the information services employ cameramen to record scenes of generosity. Crates of condensed milk are photographed in mid-air, swinging from the derrick which is to lower them on the quayside. Angle shots reveal the tractors in the hold. In this way the inhabitants of undeveloped countries are to find themselves prosperous, learning to identify their new prosperity with American aid, American manufactures and the American Way of Life.

To take these assumptions in order, there is possibly something in the idea that the more prosperous peoples are less inclined toward communism. It is apt to take root, one might argue, among groups of people who have reasons (although not always economic reasons) for discontent. A policy of economic aid may to that extent be justified on both political and humanitarian grounds, but the most effective aid for this purpose would be to offer a generous price for the undeveloped country's exports. If the progress of communism in Southeast Asia were to be checked by economic means (which is extremely improbable), a high price for rubber and tin would be the best means available. But that is not the method which America approves. Business interests in Akron and Pittsburgh offer only a low price for rubber and tin while giving tacit consent to a separate program of economic aid. The rubber is bought cheaply but the planter is consoled by the gift of an American bulldozer, free. Were the bulldozer to come from France the scheme would have at least the merit of aiding both Europe and Asia, but the bulldozer tends to come from Detroit. The policy involved is capable, therefore, of more than one interpretation. Is the real object to "dump" American manufactures which might not otherwise find a market, training Asian mechanics to use and demand a particular brand of machine while patiently awaiting the day when they will have the money to pay for a replacement? Is the whole program an indirect subsidizing of the American motor industry? In point of fact, American motives are more kindly (and more muddled) than other people are apt to suppose. But the doubt is there and so are those who are eager to express it.

Come now to the next assumption. Granted that the aid given springs, and obviously springs, from only the purest motives, are the recipients likely to register a gratitude which readily turns into friendship? Or is gratitude a more plausible explanation for hostility? Members of the Hoover Commission expressed a healthy skepticism on this point, pointing out that "neither countries nor individuals relish being kept in a dependent status by gifts." This is profoundly true and has been true indeed since those classical times when the Romans had a phrase to cover it. At an early period of American history the same idea was put memorably in these words:

> . . . It is folly in one nation to look for disinterested favors from another; that it must pay with a portion of its independence for whatever it may accept under that character; that by such acceptance, it may place itself in the condition of having given equivalents for nominal favors, and yet of being reproached with ingratitude for not giving more. There can be no greater error than to expect or calculate upon real favors from nation to nation. It is an illusion which experience must cure, which a just pride ought to discard.

So wrote George Washington in words that it would be difficult to better.

Many Americans have taken a course in how to make friends and influence people. Without suggesting that they have cause to demand their money back, we might fairly urge some change in the syllabus. From the listed methods of gaining friendship let us delete, once and for all, the method of ostentatious generosity. For friendship is possible only between equals. If there is an object in making and keeping the friendship of the Turks, it can best be done by expressing American gratitude to *them*. Is it asking too much to expect Americans to buy their tobacco and prefer it to Virginian? Perhaps it is, in which case the same result might be achieved by telling them that their troops were the best that fought in the Korean campaign, or best anyway in the attack, a compliment which would have the additional merit of being strictly true. A country's foreign policy is mainly based, of course, on its permanent interests, and to no small extent on its geographical position; but in so far as sentiment comes into it at all, more is achieved by a sincere compliment than by any number of tractors.

If there is danger in attempting to arouse feelings of gratitude, if gifts are best conveyed by sleight of hand, the money spent on United States propaganda is largely thrown away. As against that, we should be wrong to overlook the value of information centers set up in foreign capitals. These play a vital part in international affairs. The current practice is to make these as central and conspicuous as possible, fronted with plate glass, stuffed with gaily covered literature and adorned with enlarged pictures of the current President or Prime Minister. The result is that the populace can express its feelings in moments of exasperation, smashing the glass, burning the leaflets and jumping on the portraiture. This spares the windows of the Embassy itself, which is tactically sited in a back street and unrecognized even by those who pass it every day. Paragraphs about the functional use of plate glass are to be found in the pages of any architectural journal; and this is perhaps the explanation of what that queer phrase can be taken to mean.

A final point about foreign aid is that it is given too often without strings attached. Most of the money is worse than wasted, but some good might result from the conditions which might be imposed. Any aid sent to Britain, for example, would have been of incalculable value if made conditional on one thing; that all British departments of government should henceforth keep and produce a proper set of accounts. And what condition could be more reasonable? Who would lend money to a firm which produced no comprehensible balance sheet? And why should a government be treated differently? Apart, however, from the reasonable nature of the condition, no grant or loan could in itself be as valuable to Britain as would this compulsion to put its Treasury in order.

But while the United States are far ahead of Britain in having accepted a system of cost accounting, they are still responsible for waste on a staggering scale and at every level. Thus, the United States own, or owned until recently, 838 million acres of land, and storage space (mostly covered) equal to about twice the size of Manhattan Island. It is doubtful whether more than a fraction of this real estate is needed. The armed services have been united under the Department of Defense, but they still duplicate where they should combine. They maintain separate half-utilized air transportation services and separate half-empty hospitals, competing with each other for supplies. Added to these major items of waste are a host of installations and plants which were started for some good reason but which continue to exist when the occasion is past. It so happens, for example, that the federal government owns the world's largest amphitheater, built near Washington as part of a Sesquicentennial Freedom Fair which failed to take place in 1950. It seems to have cost $500,000 or thereabouts, leading only to further expense on a pageant, which was actually performed but at a heavy loss; after which (the author is assured) the Rock Creek woods were silent once more and have so remained.

One of the most spectacular examples of American waste is the Farm Support Program. Incredible as it may seem, the United States Government each year buys up untold quantities of farm produce which it can neither distribute nor use. To dump mountains of wheat upon for-

eign countries would be an act almost equivalent to war and scarcely less disruptive of the entire international economy. Nor is there any accepted plan for disposing of the surplus eggs and butter which, for lack of any better storage facilities, are presently stored in caves about the American countryside. It has even been seriously suggested that the federal government should use the Arctic icecap as its deep-freeze. Though imagination boggles at the sums paid to farmers for unwanted produce, few politicians, Democrat or Republican, have offered a workable (or at least acceptable) solution to this problem. In the meanwhile, the process of accumulation is a nightmare reminiscent of the sorcerer's apprentice, but a nightmare from which there seems to be no awakening.

On a more intimate and comprehensible scale, one of the author's correspondents lovingly recalls the procedure for handling a Government Air bill of lading during World War II. There were to be thirteen copies in all. No. 1 mailed to the recipient, Nos. 2 and 3 put on the file, Nos. 4, 5, and 6 to go in the package, No. 7 to Air Express, No. 8 to the nearest Bureau office, and so forth. What particularly impressed the critic, in this case, was that, while there were detailed instructions for disposing of No. 13, No. 12 was merely to be destroyed. Does this sort of thing still go on? It clearly does, and years of Hoovering will not remove the dust. The fact is that outside intervention can only have a limited success. The mechanics (and, above all, the incentive) for ensuring economy needs to be built into the organization itself.

Federal waste is repeated at the state and city levels. In New York, for example, the state legislature will cheerfully vote $75,000 to prepare (merely to *prepare*) for the state's participation in the 1960 White House Conference on Children and Youth. Nor is this more futile than the employment of oil inspectors in Indiana, men paid to test kerosene for flash point despite the fact that kerosene has been perfectly safe for years. It is admittedly invidious to single out one state for criticism but if we did the choice would certainly fall on the state of Omega, the last state to join the Union and the one which has caused almost insuperable difficulty in rearranging the stars and stripes. The leading politicians of Omega are Governor O'Tooley and his Democratic supporters Oratorio, O'Brien, Adagio, O'Higgins, Fortissimo and O'Shamus; and their Republican opponents Spaghetti, Sullivan, Macaroni, Murphy, Vermicelli and Donovan. At Washington the state of Omega is

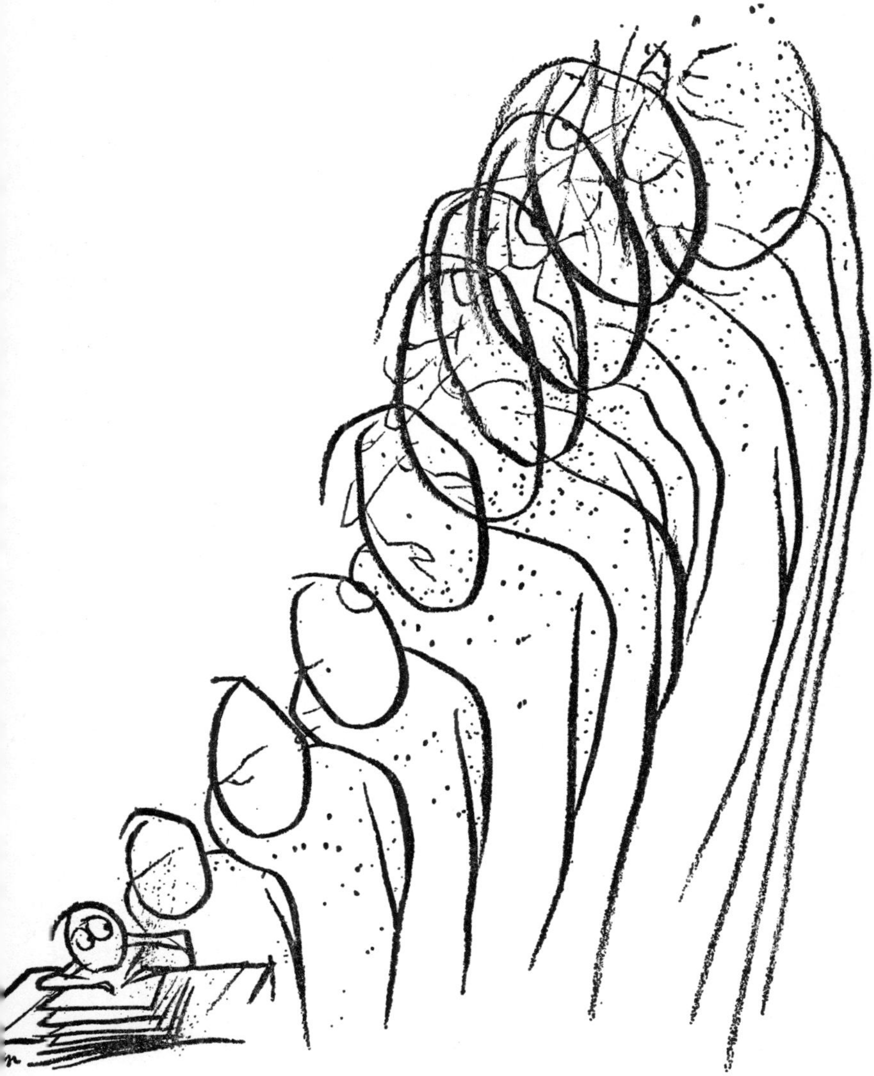

well represented by Senator Dimwit, of an old New England family. State Treasurer is Multabene Obbligato. Head of the Public Works Department is that rather controversial figure, Benito Risotto. Chief of Police is Mike O'Hara. State Auditor is Poco Pianissimo. Round Clewless City, the state capital, the rumor goes that the number of O's in the Democratic representation is reflected in the number of O's which appear in the state budget. This is hotly denied by the Democrats who allege that expenditure was even higher in the days of the Republican Governor, Alto Contralto. Be that as it may, Omega's last state budget reached the total of $434 million. A proportion of this staggering figure was due, we must admit, to such a series of odd coincidences as can surely never recur. A housing contract fixed at $14,480 had mysteriously become $232,247 before the work was completed. Some $16 million went to "consultants" and no one could discover who they were, what they were being consulted about or why. It is only fair to add that an estimate for $45,000 to be spent on a Commission for the Audit of State Needs was rejected amidst public uproar. The line has to be drawn somewhere, even in Omega.

As for Clewless City, it is like many another American metropolis. Downtown Clewless (Deadurbia) is a sort of ghost city from which merchants and retailers have mostly fled, their place being taken by immigrants from Porto Povro. A few banks and offices stand forlornly among a tangle of skyways and parking lots. Outside the rotting core of the place comes an inner circle of factories and garages, muddle and mess, overhung by drifting clouds of smog. Outside that again comes an outer residential circle (Suburbia) in which flat-lot split-level ranch houses alternate with super-markets, super-theaters and other superlatives. Outside the whole, dotted here and there, are the remote residential districts (Exurbia) of which Spectorskiland is the most fashionable. These are so remote as to be included in other states such as Disconnecticut and Paine. Families of the more successful exurbanites never visit Clewless City and the younger generation (who learn no geography) could not even tell you where it is. But the apparent decay of Clewless is not reflected in the size of the City-County Budget, which reached last year the respectable total of $120 million. One of the items which has aroused some interest is the cost of maintaining a drawbridge over the James River for the benefit of the one barge which could not otherwise pass above the bridge. Other items worthy of study are the losses on the water supply and the alleged state of the police.

Nor is Clewless altogether exceptional. If it were, we should find it difficult to explain how the amphitheater and orchestral shell built at the southern terminus of the East River Drive, New York, came to be neglected for the first ten years of its existence. Nor would it be true to say that the rural areas are less wasteful. There are seventy individual and ineffective police forces in a single county of New Guernsey and as many or more in Unaware County, Billaphobia. And the roads which connect all these places are tending to cost 18 per cent rather than 5 per cent on overheads simply through refusal to contract for the work. Bureaucracy and waste are everywhere inseparable.

A final and unnoticed result of government squandermania is that it corrupts by example. If government habitually overspends, why should the individual keep within his income? If government extravagance leads to inflation, why should anyone trouble to save? Better to spend the money before its value declines. Best of all, indeed, to be in debt, for the dollar you borrowed is worth more than the dollar you repay. Influenced thus by example and reason, the American citizen has become a permanent debtor. This has long been so but in past years the debts were more or less secured. In the instance of a refrigerator bought on the installment plan, it could at least be said that the refrigerator existed. But the present trend is to offer credit in respect of hotel accommodation, clothes, restaurant meals, holiday expenses and things which are of the stuff that dreams are made of, and leave no wrack behind. A future slump will be a slump indeed. But why should the citizen be solvent when his government is bankrupt? To be deeply in debt, in the car-strangled manner, is essential, it would seem, to the American Way of Life.

12

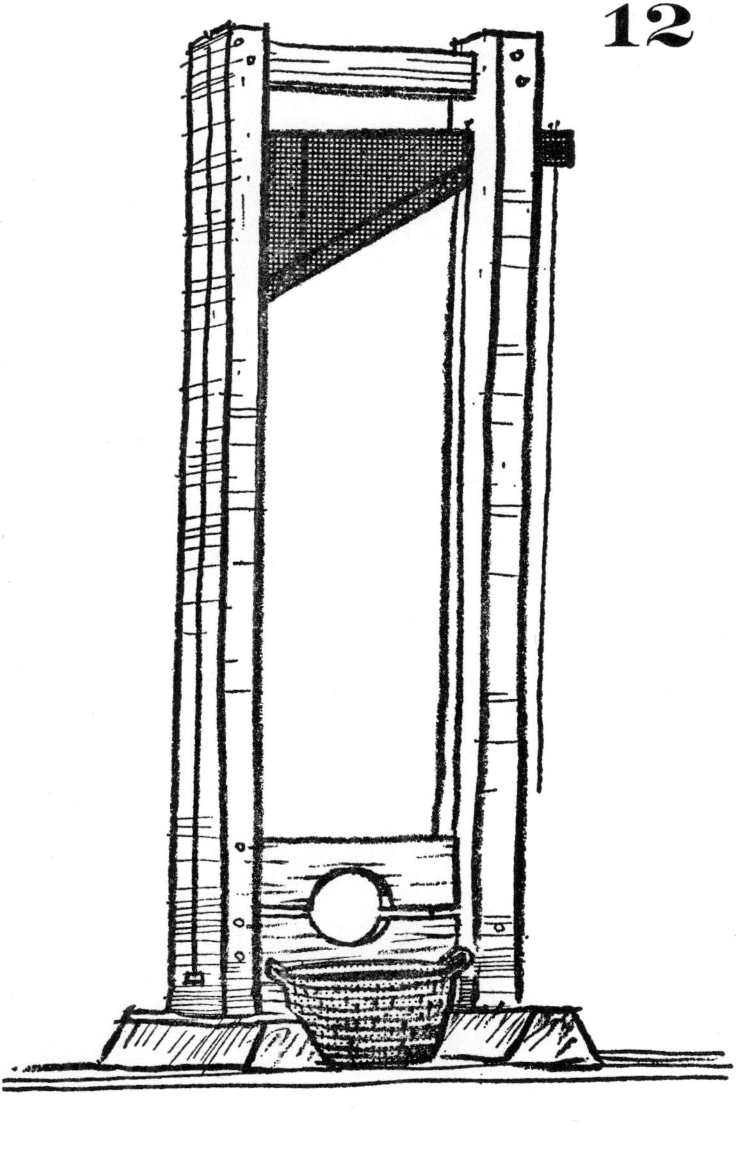

THE DANGER POINT

WORK expands to fill the time available. Administrators multiply. Governmental expenditure rises to meet and exceed public revenue. Of all this the result is, inevitably, a vast increase in the share which government takes of the national resources. The effect of governmental expansion is to absorb more and more of the national energy, initiative, ability and income; and the effect of a crushing taxation is to drive out of the country all the resources that it does not absorb.

Contemplating astronomic figures of revenue and fantastic figures of waste, the embittered taxpayer begins to regard taxation as theft. That is where he is tempted to go wrong, for taxation as such is vital to civilization. Public expenditure is justifiable for a number of necessary and even noble purposes. That the citizen should contribute toward the common defense, toward the dignity of the state, toward the maintenance of justice and order is not seriously open to dispute. He owes a debt to the state as well as to his ancestors and descendants. He was brought up under its protection, induced to obey its laws, taught to rely on its justice and endowed with a share of its fame. Only the stateless know what it is to have no national legend, pride or flag. For the privileges of citizenship the individual must pay. Up to a point, moreover, the value of the privileges must depend upon the amount and readiness of his payment. For the state without revenue is a state without power. Demanding little, it has little, in turn, to give.

The proper amount of the revenue and the just assessment of the tax are problems, essentially, of proportion. As between the point where the citizen gives nothing and the point where the state takes all there is, somewhere, the golden mean. Earlier in this book some attempt was made to show where taxation becomes excessive and dan-

gerous. It would have been easier, perhaps, though less practically useful, to fix a point below which taxation must be thought insufficient. But as the tendency is always in the one direction, the problem must center upon the point at which, with taxes rising, we must agree to call a halt. Were this problem solved with any degree of finality, our civilization's peril would be less. To convince all that such a point of danger exists, falling between this percentage and that, would need perhaps a bigger volume than this and from a more illustrious pen. But there is space yet to discuss some of the symptoms by which we can judge how near to disaster we have already come. Even were we to reject all percentages and graphs, arguing, as some economists do, that no two countries are alike, there are other indications which are enough in themselves to convey a warning. There is social as well as international disaster and we have good reason to believe that Britain is very near the brink.

The danger signs appear in this order: First, it becomes apparent that government is absorbing too great share of the available talent and energy; there is a decline, therefore, in individual initiative and the spirit of inertia takes its place. Second, there is a decline in the sense of property, and the spirit of envy takes its place. Third, there is a decline of freedom, and the spirit of dependence takes its place. Fourth, there is a decline in the sense of purpose and the spirit of rebellion takes its place. All this adds up to a decline in the sense of individual responsibility, and so to a decline of individuality itself. And while the technical trend of the age goes to make the individual matter more, politically the trend is to make him matter less. In this grinding of the individual to nothingness, the most effective instrument is the steam roller of taxation. Under its pressure the individual is merged into the mass.

Take, first of all, the demands of government on the national resources of trained intelligence and drive. In times past the promising graduate was supposed to make his choice between public service and private enterprise. The civil service offered him security and public recognition, slow promotion and moderate pay. Industry or commerce offered him greater but more precarious rewards, swifter rise but a position less assured. And this is still the contrast as pictured by many of the elderly or ill informed. That it is totally false is being realized by the few. In point of fact, the civil service has added to its original attractions the lure of quick promotion and generous pay. The successful administrator in an expanding service expects to make £2500 to £3000 a year, knighthood complete, at the age of about forty-five. From that point he can either rise to become Permanent Secretary, with £6000 or £7000 a year, or aim at an early retirement with tax-free gratuity, perquisites and pension. Without discussing what all this costs the taxpayer, the point we must notice is that the rewards in business, while still precarious, are less. Directorships are more slowly achieved, more easily lost and less generously paid. Now that the civil servant is given a higher salary than the Minister under whose direction he is supposed to work, and now that the attractions of the career are beginning to be realized, the tendency must be, and clearly is, for the ablest young men to seek their fortune in Whitehall rather than in the City.

In this tendency there is both good and ill. With so much responsibility given to administrators, there is some merit in a plan which ensures that the administrators are the best available; and better than ever in that India no longer claims the best of all. So far as administrative efficiency goes, the most one can say in general criticism is that the civil service is more successful in recruiting talent than in developing the talent that it has. Leaders are neither created nor eliminated by the processes of public administration. While the best are promoted, the useless are retained. In the Navy, the Air Force or in business, there is a natural selection at work. The patrol craft on the sandbank, the jet bomber buried in the hillside and the firm gone bankrupt all represent careers checked or terminated. There are no equivalent risks in government, no system by which men are either broken or made.

But the possible failings of the bureaucrat are the least of the dangers in bureaucracy. The greatest danger rises specifically from the bureaucrat's success. The more implicitly we rely upon his honesty and intelligence, the less we rely upon ourselves. Instead of calling forth the energies of the people an entrenched bureaucracy offers its own energy as a substitute. How far this tendency had gone was apparent in the early days of World War II. The prewar concept had been that government would do all. Tanks and guns would come not from factories but from ordnance depots. Industrialists were told to mind their own business. Unofficial efforts to help were rather discouraged than welcomed. The Observer Corps, which was obviously essential, met with departmental opposition and was actually financed at first from private funds. No attempt was made to discover where the country's key points were — the centers where air attack would cause the maximum dislocation. When the problem arose of utilizing the country's industrial resources, the Ministry of Supply did not even know where the factories were or what they did. Nor did the Ministry of Labour know what the population amounted to. As for the system of roof spotters, which was to play a vital part in maintaining production, it began as an individual effort without official approval or aid. When it came, last of all, to ensuring essential supplies of food and of tin containers, the war began before the orders for them had even been placed.

The concept of an exclusive war did not survive for long the experience of actual conflict. Government, it was found, when left to itself, manufactured little but delay. The strength or weakness of the existing bureaucracy could be measured indeed by the time which elapsed before it was swept aside. The system has since reappeared, however, and we are told, in effect, that government will think for us and spend for us. More than that, government will recruit the ablest among us and use their services in the best possible way. In considering the advantages and drawbacks of this plan we should do well to remember that administrative ability is far less specialized than most people suppose. There are certain people — ventriloquists, operatic tenors, pugilists and trapeze artists — whose abilities can be used only in a certain way. Bureaucrats are not, however, among them. The man who can govern a prison might as readily, perhaps, have edited a newspaper. A man who succeeded as a novelist was successful again in governing Canada. Another who designed aircraft went on from there to write novels. So that it is perfectly possible for a government to recruit many able young men whose abilities might as readily have been used in another direction. And in some countries, at a certain stage of their development, there might be little objection to this concentration of effort. In Russia, perhaps, or China, there might be good reason to marshal all available talent in the public service; and the eventual result might be held to justify the temporary inconvenience. But the argument which might hold good in a self-sufficient country is inapplicable to a country which must export to live. Goods for export do not come from official out-trays but from individual effort. From the point of view, therefore, of economic survival, the successful civil servant may matter a great deal less than a writer of fairy stories for children. There are drawbacks, therefore, in a system which lavishes favor on the bureaucrat while driving the potential exporter to take refuge overseas.

The extent to which the national effort has been channeled into the public services is a matter not of supposition but of fact. In 1956 the following numbers of people were on the British payroll:

Civil Service	386,000
Post Office	252,000
N.H.S. Physicians	39,000
Health Services	380,000
Ordnance Factories	120,000
Naval Shipyards	100,000
	1,277,000

On the local government payroll there were:

Local government	1,556,000
Teachers	316,000
Police	76,000
Health services	142,000
	2,090,000

Employed in nationalized industries there were:

Railways	566,000
Coal	783,000
Electricity & Gas	378,000
Docks	80,000
	1,807,000

Here then are 5,174,000 civilians in government, local government or semi-government employ. The addition of the armed forces and some miscellaneous groups would bring the total to about 6,000,000. Out of a population of 51,613,000, as estimated, this is no small proportion, amounting in fact to almost one in eight. These figures are only very approximate, for several reasons. To begin with, the numbering of the civil service is difficult, there being a dubious fringe of those partly employed. And then the population is an unknown quantity, so much so that different departments were working on quite different estimates during World War II, with perhaps two million people overlooked by the Ministry of Labour. But with all inaccuracies admitted, it remains roughly true that mere administration absorbs nearly two million people, one out of every twenty-six persons and one out of every eleven adults below the age of retirement. Not all those publicly employed are unproductive. Administration is, however, a dwindling British export, and those engaged in it are not contributing directly to the total of what Britain has to sell. The burden of this multitude weighs heavily on the initiative and enterprise of the few.

Confronted with such figures as these, the ordinary citizen must have his moments of gloom. Nor will he become more cheerful as a result of studying the Parliamentary Sessional Papers. He may, it is true, gain the impression that the Select Committee on the Estimates is opposed, in general, to extravagance. The Committee, he may note, went so far as to comment upon the £40 million wasted on Swift aircraft, the £16 million wasted on combat vehicles, and even upon the comparable wastage on Solent flying boats. The Committee's reports are not, he will find, without their note of regret. They sometimes include phrases which come near to expressing disapproval. It was evidently felt among the members that £50 or £60 million might comprise a sum large enough to be missed. Nothing in themselves perhaps, these trifling losses would, if repeated, add up eventually to a considerable sum. The Committee had evidently in mind the words of the old proverb, look after the millions and the billions will look after themselves. But any momentary consolation to be derived from the thought that there is one Committee on the taxpayer's side is lost again in the realization that all these comments concern sums which are lost and gone forever. Little can be done, it would seem, to prevent the losses that are still to come. These seem to be at once inevitable and immense.

It is a study of the tax outlook that saps initiative and encourages inertia. There may be some handful of people who find inspivation (a recently invented term) in a jungle of regulations to evade, and of these some few will have seen how to use inflation for their own purpose. For the majority, the prospect is merely disheartening. Why extend or develop the business? More trade means more trouble but no greater income. It was noticed, some years

ago, in the Department of Inland Revenue, that a certain great landowner was failing to collect his rents. Some farmers paid him, others refrained, and it made no difference to him whether they paid or not. He was therefore admonished. "My Lord Duke," said the tax authorities, "you must collect your rents." To this he replied tersely, "Collect them yourselves." This is an extreme case, where the cost of collection came to more than the rent (after tax) was worth. But the same inertia has spread right down through society until the workman comes to shorten his week, keeping his wages to a level at which the tax is minimized. Initiative has largely died away and the spirit of inertia has taken its place.

Next, there is a decline in the sense of property. It cannot be otherwise, for the whole idea of private property

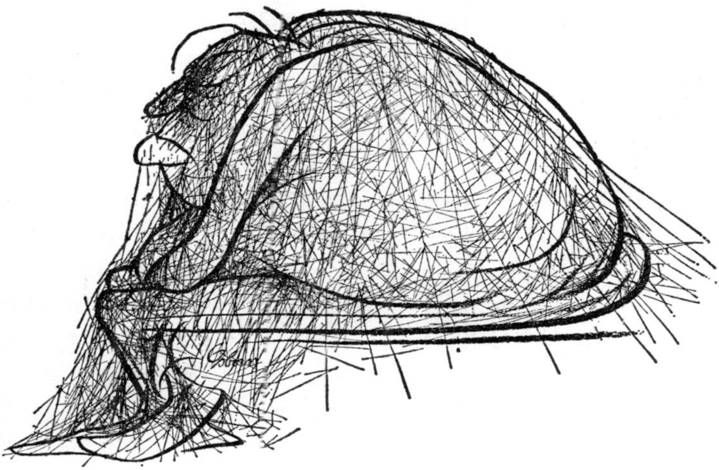

rests upon the assumption that it cannot be confiscated. It may be taken from a convicted criminal or it may be requisitioned for purposes of defending the realm but it should be, in general, sacrosanct. Nor is taxation, up to a point, inconsistent with individual ownership. The income is liable to tax but the estate still belongs to the owner. But with the assessment of tax at over 50 per cent and the imposition of death duties at (say) 75 per cent, ownership becomes no more than a precarious tenure. The state owns all but concedes something to the individual; a something, moreover, which can be varied at will. In these circumstances all sense of ownership has gone, and with it all sense of permanence. And there are many who welcome this loss, considering that the individual has no right to such a vested interest as real ownership must imply. Others will question whether the individual is not, in fact, freer and happier when relieved of his inheritance. To many the abolition of private property is an unmixed good.

In arguments of this kind there is a measure of truth. When we see old etchings in which country houses are depicted as if from the air, we feel that seventeenth-century family pride could go quite far enough. There may be an unerring sense of proportion about the architecture but the landscape seems too often to have got out of hand. No one is to be grudged his wrought-iron gates, but should they be approached by an avenue four miles long? And what if the avenues converge from all points of the compass, making a nobleman's mansion the very center of his county and probably of his universe? Combined with the aesthetic merits of this plan there must seem to be a hint of lunacy. Is it healthy for a single family to be, or even to think itself, as important as that? Historically, this egotism could be justified. The story of the British Empire could be retold in terms of the country house, showing how its avenues were extended until the vice-regal lodge gates came to be located in Dublin, Williamsburg and Calcutta. But the uneasy feeling remains that grandeur can be carried too far.

It is also undoubtedly true that some heirs to great estates have felt imprisoned by magnificence and oppressed by the overpowering past. They have grown up to discover that their house belongs to the butler and housekeeper, their flower beds to the head gardener, their woods to the gamekeeper and everything else to the estate agent. Reading family prayers because it was Grandmother's custom, dressing for dinner because it was Father's wish, hunting because it is the proper thing to do and shooting because it is the proper time of year, many a nobleman has longed for the freedom of Miami or Capri. Death duties have been a relief to some, an excuse for pensioning servants and giving the Rembrandts to the nation. At last they have felt free to seek refuge in Bermuda or Antibes, playing with speedboats or riding the surf.

Granted, however, that private property can become a sort of mania and that the reaction against it can take a form still less admirable, the fact remains that its destruction will leave us with a world become colorless, aimless and dull. The unanswerable argument for property is aesthetic. There is, in many or most people, an innate longing for beauty and order. For some this desire is satisfied by a fitted carpet in the parlor or by wallflowers in the windowbox. But when prosperity goes beyond this point, expenditure can take one or two forms. It can provide either for the pleasure of the moment or for a permanent asset in the years to come. The momentary pleasures include those of sex, spectacle, gambling, drink and speed. They also include such admirable things as travel, danger and listening to classical music. The more permanent pleasures include marriage, children, houses, gardens, furniture, carpets, trees and shrubs. In a normally balanced life there should be room for both the momentary and the lasting pleasure. The same person can enjoy painting a gate or hearing an opera. But it is generally felt, and rightly, that the sense of balance should be there. The young man obsessed with gambling and the old lady obsessed with Dresden china are not only both mistaken but are guilty of the same mistake. They have lost their sense of proportion.

In an age of penal taxation and death duties this sense of

proportion is difficult to retain. For every argument of common sense is on the side of the ephemeral pleasure and against any sort of acquired asset. During the present century the best investment has been, unquestionably, travel. To have been to Bokhara or Sarawak, to Peking or Cuba, is to have gained something not subject to assessment. Your experience is something that cannot be taken from you. It can, moreover, appreciate in value with the tax-caused process of inflation. To visit Bali next year would probably cost more than to go there now and might not even be possible. The place visited may even virtually cease to exist. Thus the man who can say "I remember, in Shanghai, in the old days . . ." is fully entitled to his dreamy expression. He has something which his younger friends must simply do without. No one, surely, has ever regretted any recent expenditure on travel. But one's attitude is the same toward the ephemeral in any form. A night in Bangkok, an evening in Hong Kong, a lost week-end in Paris or a day at the races are alike in this, that they leave behind no taxable asset. The wreath of flowers dropped at dawn into the ship's wake off Tahiti may, in itself, be no proof of sobriety and virtue, but no one has yet tried to assess it under Schedule D. The wine has been drunk and the girls have grown old but there is nothing left to tax.

In the last days of the Roman Empire (or in the Singapore, for that matter, of 1942) there was a natural urge to drink the wine while it was there. Unless we admit, however, that our situation is exactly the same, we have sound reasons for thinking that such an attitude would (for us) be wrong. We should keep our sense of proportion. There are reasons, moreover, for concluding that the balance should tip, if at all, on the side of the long-term and heritable pleasure. These reasons are basically arithmetic. Suppose the choice should lie between a week at Cannes and a marble statuette for the garden, the one will give pleasure to us alone but the other (we may hope) to our neighbors, descendants and guests. But the marble faun at the end of the grasswalk, white against the evergreens, is subject to death duties. So are the classical pillars and so are the mullioned windows through which the light gleams at dusk. Death duties are levied on the stone-flagged terrace and the Georgian candelabra, on the gilded clockface and almost, one might add, on the cooing of the doves. Warmly as the sun may light the threshold, the shadow of the tax collector falls ghastly on the checkered marble floor. Why should we strive to create what none can inherit, or plant the trees which none will live to see?

The menace of the tax collector is no idle figure of speech. After the death, recently, of a distinguished author, the Estate Duty Office raised the valuation on his house by £4500. The executors employed an eminent estate agent, through whose efforts this valuation was reduced again to something like the original figure. The Estate Duty Office then tried to put a value on the film rights of a novel that had not yet been filmed; a hypothetical value on something which was proved to be unsalable. Defeated on this issue, their next move was to challenge the valuation of the copyrights, seeking to fix a sum greater than a famous publishing house was prepared to offer and more than an eminent literary agent was prepared to ask. The expense of all this negotiation, the fees to solicitors, valuers and experts, could come only out of the disputed estate. Finally, the Estate Duty Office claimed interest on the duty that had not been paid because it had not even been agreed. The idea of private property is all but dead.

What has taken its place? Its place has been taken by the spirit of envy. Behind the whole philosophy of taxation there lurk two distinct ideas. On the one hand is the notion that the taxation of the rich may directly benefit the poor, giving them the food, shelter, warmth and medical care which they would otherwise lack. The dangers in this plan are obvious, more especially if the votes of the poor are to decide on the extent to which this assistance should be provided. Granted, however, that these dangers exist, it can still be argued that the general purpose is benevolent. It can

be urged that people ought not to lack these elementary needs and that, with modern productiveness, there is no reason why they should. Of this argument it can at least be said that people's reasonable wants are the object in view. In contrast with this, on the other hand, is the quite different argument that the taxation of the more prosperous reduces the scope for envy. The discomforts of relative poverty are thus to be lessened by the removal of relative wealth. By this reasoning the undermining of established prosperity is a good in itself, quite apart from any use to which the money may be put. Taxation for this purpose panders to some of the least creditable motives of which the human mind is capable.

The envy felt by those who are not in want is not only odious but stupid. As it is impossible for everyone to own a Rolls-Royce, the factory should be closed and the existing cars sold for scrap. If there is insufficient salmon and grouse for everybody, there should be none for anybody. If champagne is not available for all, it should be drunk by none. But this is absurd. There can be no sense in pouring wine down the sink merely because there is not enough of it. And what is absurd when applied to wine becomes lunatic when applied to architecture. No one else is a penny the worse off because the Duke of Westminster's gates are gilded. Indeed, we are the better off and could admire them (if we chose) more often than does he. No one should be impoverished by the thought that the Marquess of Bath owns all the treasures of Longleat. Someone has to own them, and why not the man to whom they happen to belong? In all this sort of envy there is a revolting compound of all the meanest sentiments, mixed with the crudest ignorance and garnished with the most nauseating deceit.

Were British fiscal policy influenced mainly by a desire to benefit the poor, there would be much to be said against the sentimentality involved. But with all the vote-catching dishonesties which such a campaign must imply there would be included some trace of humanitarian values. There would be something in it for which one could feel respect. The fact is, however, that fiscal policy is guided rather by the second set of motives, by the spirit of envy. Proof of this lies in those final brackets of surtax which affect the merest handful of people. To reduce tax at those highest levels from 95 per cent to 75 per cent would deprive the revenue of only a negligible sum, would leave no one the poorer and might save some ancient castles from demolition or sale. But those last fiscal severities were imposed and are retained, not for any sound financial reason, not for the appreciable benefit of anybody but simply and solely to satisfy the malice of those whose minds have room for little else. If finance based on sentiment is bad, how much worse is a finance based on mere envy.

Next we must observe a decline in the sense of freedom. Its place has been taken by the spirit of dependence. In past centuries, to deprive a man of his estate was the punishment for some of the blackest crimes. To drive him, as an outlaw, into exile might be the fit reward of treason. To-day these punishments fall on those who have committed no offense. More than that, they fall on those who have rendered the highest service to the state. To this a defender of the system might rejoin that hard cases make bad law and that individuals must suffer for the common good. Whatever may be thought of a justice so devised, the question rises as to whether the common good is really served. Injustice to one leads to the restriction of freedom for all.

With freedom lessened, what of the common good remains?

To this question some would answer that the working classes have willingly traded freedom for security. It can further be argued that deduction of the tax from the pay envelope leaves many people unaware of the tax they have to pay. In all of this there is some truth. But it is a question whether the current security is really very secure. As a smaller country, with much of its overseas investment gone, Britain's chief asset lies in her stock of ability. Other countries have larger populations, richer resources, wider territories and greater power. To retain any sort of position in the world the British must rely chiefly upon their experience, integrity, enterprise, knowledge and skill. Of these resources too great a proportion are absorbed in government or in the battles of tax avoidance. Something remains, however, and with it much should be possible. But these are the very assets which the tax system tends to destroy. Experience is vested in families which have devoted centuries of application to commerce, finance, investment and law. Integrity is invested in banks and firms and merchant houses. For enterprise we look to our inventors, explorers, technicians and artists; to our men of imagination, perseverance, vision and drive. For knowledge we look to our scholars, scientists and authors, for skill to our navigators, engineers and craftsmen. But those are the very people we penalize, persecute and drive overseas. Unluckily, these losses are invisible. Who can measure a decline in integrity? Who can enumerate the inventions that have not been made, the books that have not been written, the enterprises which have never taken place, the careers not even begun? The loss to the country is not

less real for being intangible. With freedom gone, much else is lost besides.

With the weakening of a sense of initiative, of property, of freedom, there goes inevitably a loss of purpose. In times past the poor family could work toward some reasonable goal; to own their own farm, to buy their own shop, to place one son in the priesthood or send one girl to school. But much of what is attainable has now become worthless. The farmer may be less prosperous than the mechanic, the shopkeeper poorer than the plumber's helper. To be a teacher is nothing and to be a clergyman is less. For many families all sense of purpose has been lost, but with results more observable in the children than in the parents. For it is against this purposeless life that the younger folk are tending to rebel. Much has been written and much remains to write about the adolescents of today; about teen-age delinquents, switchblade knives and bloodshed. But of one thing we can be certain; these are the first products of the Welfare State. Theirs is not a background of illiteracy, unemployment, sweated labor and want. They are children who, by comparison with earlier generations, have been given everything except a purpose in life. After having medical attention, food, schooling and exercise, they display energies which previous adolescents seem to have lacked. The world they are offered is unbearably tedious. Having no struggle for survival and being thoroughly bored with their surroundings, the young invent a world of their own; and very repulsive it is. Upon the Welfare State, upon the whole idea of the tax-gathering utopia, the juvenile delinquent provides the final comment. He derides the present age as dull. And dull, for him, is exactly what it is.

TAX
Osborn

CONCLUSION

THE FIRST TASK of a government should be to decide upon the proportion which they can safely take of the national income. In time of emergency, with the national existence at stake, the proportion can be high. At other times it should be low, allowing scope for increase when a crisis should arise. What, in normal circumstances, should that proportion be?

History tells us that governments of the more remote past have tended to exact about 10 per cent of the people's income. We learn, further, that tax demands above that level have often driven people to emigrate, at least in circumstances where migration was possible. Where flight has been for some reason impracticable, taxes of 20 per cent or more have been collected without much difficulty. As against that, taxes rising from 33 to 50 per cent have been the occasion for revolt or the cause of ruin. Taxes fixed at these high levels have characterized regimes of dwindling importance, their decay in strength being accompanied by decline of their literature and arts. During the present century, levels of taxation have risen toward the point at which previous disaster has been known to occur. Populations which have become largely literate are exposed to modern methods of tax collection which are based upon their literacy and upon their inability to escape. Democracy has given political power to those who, taxed themselves at the lower rate, will gladly support the penal taxation of the wealthy. The result has been the disproportionate or progressive system of direct taxation by which fortunes are largely confiscated. Taxation of this kind can be pushed to any extreme and there is at present no accepted level at which its upper limit can be fixed. It is currently assumed, rather, that the amount of revenue to be raised will be related in some way to the estimated total of public expenditure.

The drawback in thus attempting to adjust revenue to expenditure is that all expenditure rises to meet income. Parkinson's Second Law, a matter of common knowledge so far as the individual's finances are concerned, is also applicable to the government. But whereas the individual's expenses rise to meet and perhaps exceed an income level which is at least known, government expenditure rises in the same way toward a maximum that has never been defined; toward a ceiling that is not there. It rises, therefore, unchecked, toward levels which past experience has shown to be disastrous. In several modern countries the symptoms of approaching catastrophe are already obvious; and in none more so than in Britain. But this is not a matter in which Americans can afford to feel complacent.

They are moving in the same direction even if they have not gone as far. They too have failed to fix a limit beyond which taxation must not go.

Where should the peacetime limit be drawn? It should be fixed at 20 per cent of the national income, well short of the point (25 per cent) at which the tax will cause inflation and further from the point (30 per cent) at which a country's international influence must begin to decline. From such a peacetime level the taxes can be safely raised in time of war, provided only that they are reduced again when the conflict ends. The perpetual danger, however, is that the wartime tax level will be afterwards maintained — peacetime expenditure having risen to meet it — with long-term disaster as the inevitable sequel.

To any such proposal as this, limiting national expenditure to the amount which the country can afford, there will be opposition from those who fear a reduction in the social services which they would rather see developed. How are low taxes compatible with the Welfare State? Will not cheaper government be worse? The answer is that cheaper government is better. The effect of providing government with unlimited funds is merely to clog the wheels of administration with useless officials and superfluous paper. All that we buy with higher taxes is additional administrative delay.

There are directions in which greater public expense would be fully justified — as, for instance, in the rebuilding of our obsolete cities — but this is no argument for heavier taxation. Funds for this and for every other enlightened purpose could be made available through the elimination of waste. Like taxation, waste has its origin in war. It continues after peace is made, and especially in the channels of expenditure which war has opened up. It continues as a torrent of needless expense, as a toil erosion of the deadliest kind. Waste is the enemy. It is the spectacle of public waste that seems to justify, if it does not cause, the widespread avoidance (or even evasion) of tax. It is the spectacle of public extravagance which seems to justify, if it does not cause, the nation-wide fashion in individual indebtedness. Toward serving the nobler purposes of the state, while at the same time easing the burden of taxes, an essential step is to eliminate waste; and the waste not merely of material but of talent and of time. But nothing of this sort is possible unless the whole process of public finance is reversed. There can be no economy while the public revenue is made roughly equal to the sum of the departmental demands. Economy must begin with fixing the revenue as a proportion of the national income and informing each department of the total expenditure it must not exceed. With every incentive to internal economy and with automatic dismissal following every deficit, we should soon find that much can be done with little and more, very often, can be done with less. Put an absolute limit to the revenue and then let expenditure rise to meet it. These are the profits of experience and from these profits we should derive our law.